EVERYDAY GOURMET

GERRY GALVIN's philosophy of cooking is simple: fresh ingredients and lots of imagination are the key. It's a philosophy which he has proven to work in the restaurant he and his wife Marie now run at Drimcong House in County Galway, which is a two-time winner of the Bord Fáilte/Ballygowan Supreme Award of Excellence. Gerry himself has also won many awards including the Egon Ronay Chef of the Year 1994 and Guinness Chef of the Year 1996.

Everyday Gourmet

GERRY GALVIN

Photographs by Walter Pfeiffer

THE O'BRIEN PRESS
DUBLIN

For Marie again

First published 1997 by The O'Brien Press Ltd.,
20 Victoria Road, Dublin 6, Ireland

© for text – Gerry Galvin
© for typesetting, layout, cover design, photographs – The O'Brien Press Ltd

ISBN 0-86278-537-5

British Library Cataloguing-in-Publication Data
Galvin, Gerry
The everyday gourmet
1.Cookery
I.Title II.Pfeiffer, Walter
641.5'14

1 2 3 4 5 6 7 8 9 10
97 98 99 00 01 02 03 04 05 06

This book is produced in partnership with Tesco Ireland

Typesetting, editing, layout, cover design: The O'Brien Press Ltd
Photographs: Walter Pfeiffer
Cover separations: Lithoset Ltd
Printing and separations: Proost, Belgium

CONTENTS

Introduction

Everyday Gourmet is a book of easy-to-use and, I hope, delicious recipes for all those interested in expanding their cooking repertoire. It seems to me that many cookbooks require exotic ingredients that can sometimes be hard to find. I wanted to spare would-be cooks that annoyance. With this in mind I compiled these recipes in partnership with Tesco Ireland and all the recipe ingredients can be bought in their supermarkets nationwide (Quinnsworth).

Cooking can be an adventure and, over the years, I have tried to convey that through the medium of the Drimcong Cookery Courses. Everyday Gourmet continues that quest. I also believe that food is for sustenance and about pleasure rather than rarified research, and that the cult of the super chef, whose recipes are vague, often guarded, secrets is simply absurd. Everyday Gourmet is for cooks of all levels of skill.

The nostalgic picture of families united over the dinner table fades by the day. Our furious pace of life demands faster and faster food, and 'eating-on-the-hoof' or 'grazing' are terms often used to describe modern eating habits. My hope is that Everyday Gourmet will tempt cooks to invest time and thought in preparing sensible, happy meals.

For efficient use of the recipes in the book please note the following:

1. I do not give homemade stock recipes. I assume instead that readymade ranges of stock cubes will be used where recipes indicate the use of stock. Do remember that some stock cubes have a high salt content.

2. I use a lot of fresh herbs in my cooking. Your local Tesco/Quinnsworth supermarket will be able to supply fresh-packed herbs throughout the year, varying with the seasons. If using dried rather than fresh herbs use approximately half the quantity.

3. Eggs in the recipes are medium-sized unless otherwise indicated.

4. I love cream and use it as often as possible. Those who prefer – or need – low-fat recipes can substitute crème fraîche.

5. The wine suggestions are just that – suggestions.

When planning a meal from the book, my advice is to, where possible, use foods that are in season. For example, homegrown strawberries and raspberries are vastly superior to imported ones. Our strawberry season lasts throughout the summer. Local raspberries are available in June/July. Where possible, too, use organic produce.

To conclude I want to thank all those who helped me put this book together: Marie, my wife; Frances Power, my editor; Freda Molamphy, Food Advisor, Tesco Ireland; the current staff at Drimcong, particularly chefs Mary Toher, Tony Schwarz, Martin Halissey; and Paul Fogerty for his wine suggestions. Thanks also to Walter Pfeiffer whose photographs speak for themselves.

Gerry Galvin
Drimcong House
Moycullen

SOUPS AND STARTERS

The beginning of a good lunch or dinner should be tasty, not too filling and sufficiently exciting to generate a sense of anticipation for things to come. These soups and starters give a variety of dishes to choose from and are easy to prepare in small quantities. However, there is no reason why the quantities cannot be increased to make main courses. Feel free to experiment!

Cheese Soup with Celery Sticks

4 portions

METHOD

1 In a pot over medium heat whisk together milk, cream, mustard, flour and butter. Cook and stir gently for five minutes.

2 Add cheeses and simmer for a further five minutes, stirring all the time.

3 Dilute to soup consistency with stock.

4 Whisk in salt (if required), cayenne pepper and lemon juice.

5 Pour into soup plates, sprinkle each portion with paprika and dunk a celery stick into each serving.

WINE

A Cabernet Sauvignon (red)

INGREDIENTS

700 ml/1 pt milk

50 ml/2 fl oz cream

2 tsp Dijon mustard

25 g/1 oz flour

40 g/1 ½ oz butter

50 g/2 oz grated Gruyère cheese

► 50 g/2 oz grated cheddar

► 400 ml/¾ pt vegetable stock

pinch of cayenne pepper

1 tsp fresh lemon juice

salt and paprika

4 sticks of celery, each 12 cm/5 inch long

► OPTIONS

Replace the cheddar with the same amount of blue cheese for a stronger, more cheesy flavour.

With less stock this soup becomes a cheese sauce.

Chinese Broth

INGREDIENTS

400 ml/¾ pt chicken, fish
or vegetable stock

150 ml/¼ pt dry white wine

1 tbs balsamic vinegar

3 spring onions, finely sliced

1 tbs ginger root, grated

1 tbs Chinese five-spice powder

½ tbs harissa
(see p 111) or chilli sauce

2 large garlic cloves, crushed

juice of half a lemon

salt and ground black pepper

METHOD

1 Bring stock to the boil.

2 Add all other ingredients, whisking and
simmering for three minutes.

3 Serve.

WINE

A German Riesling (white)

OPTIONS

This speedy, flavoursome broth can be
served as a soup or with other dishes
such as Chicken and Ham Dumplings
(see p 38). It could become a fish main
course with the addition of 450 g/1 lb
of mixed fish, chopped small. The fish
will cook in the boiling broth in a
matter of minutes.

Potted Pâté

4 portions
Use ramekins with 150 ml/¼ pt capacity

METHOD

1 Cut cooked meat in small pieces and process to a thick paste, gradually adding the melted butter. (This can be done in two batches, so as not to put too much strain on the food processor.)
2 Add alcohol, garlic, spice and seasoning.
3 Pack into individual ramekins and refrigerate until about 10 minutes before use.
4 Serve with thin slices of brown or white toast.

WINE

A Merlot (red)

INGREDIENTS

450 g/1 lb cold, cooked chicken, turkey or ham
275 ml/½ pt melted butter
1 ½ tbs brandy or port
2 garlic cloves, crushed
½ tsp mixed spice
salt and ground white pepper
brown or white sliced bread, toasted

▶ OPTIONS

This quick and easy pâté can be made from any left-over cooked meat. It can also be packed in one large bowl rather than individual ramekins – in which case serve it directly from the bowl with a tablespoon. Do not keep for more than a few days.

Pea Soup

INGREDIENTS

2 streaky rashers

50 g/2 oz butter

4 spring onions, chopped

2 cloves garlic, crushed

25 g/1 oz spinach leaves, fresh or frozen, chopped

450 g/1 lb frozen peas

700 ml/1 pt vegetable or chicken stock

1 tbs fresh mint, chopped

OPTIONS

Vegetarians could substitute a little of one of the savoury butters (see pp 115-116) or yoghurt for the chopped rashers.

Sometimes peas can be very sweet, in which case whisk a teaspoon of fresh lemon juice into the soup before serving.

METHOD

1 Fry or grill rashers until crisp. Cool.

2 Heat butter in a pot and add spring onions, garlic, spinach and peas.

3 Cover and cook gently for 10 minutes.

4 Add stock. Bring to the boil and simmer for five minutes.

5 Liquidise, strain through a sieve and whisk. Reheat.

6 Finely chop the rashers and sprinkle over the soup portions.

7 Sprinkle the chopped mint over each portion and serve.

WINE

A Sancerre (white)

Facing page: Pea Soup

Black Pudding and Apple on French Toast

INGREDIENTS

3 eggs

2 tbs Parmesan cheese, grated

pinch of ground cinnamon

8 slices of baguette (french bread) 1 cm/½ inch thick x 6 cm/2 ½ inch wide

50 g/2 oz butter

8 x 25 g/1 oz slices black pudding each 6 cm/2½ inch wide

2 medium dessert apples, peeled, cored and chopped small

OPTIONS

This is an appealing dish because of its simplicity and versatility – it can be used both as a savoury starter or as an unusual breakfast offering. If your favourite black pudding is less than 6 cm/2½ inch wide use extra slices to make up the weight.

METHOD

1 Beat eggs, parmesan and cinnamon very well together and coat the bread slices with this mixture, dipping and turning until completely coated.

2 Heat the butter in a large frying pan and fry the bread slices over medium heat until golden brown on both sides.

3 Remove bread from pan. Pat dry on kitchen paper and keep hot.

4 Fry the pudding slices in the same pan over the same heat for about two minutes each side. Remove and place a slice of pudding on top of each baguette slice.

5 Using the same pan, toss the apple in the remaining butter for a minute and then divide apple and butter equally over the pudding/baguette slices.

Baked Avocado with Fish Mousse and Curried Coconut Sauce

4 portions
Oven: 200°C/400°F/gas mark 6

METHOD

1 To make the mousse, blend the cold fish to a paste in a food processor.

2 Add the egg followed by the cream and sherry/wine.

3 Remove mix to a cold bowl and season with salt, pepper and nutmeg.

4 Halve and peel avocados and brush all over with lemon juice. Slice a sliver off each avocado bottom so that the avocado sits easily in a baking dish. Place the slivers in the avocado cavities.

5 Spoon or pipe mousse into each avocado half in equal quantities.

6 Brush the base of the baking dish, the avocados and mousse with butter.

7 Bake for about 10 minutes until the mousse is just firm to the touch.

8 Take the avocado halves out of the oven and sit on kitchen paper for a few seconds to drain off dripping fat and juices.

9 To make the sauce, bring the coconut milk to the boil in a small pot.

10 Boil briskly for a minute while whisking in the curry paste.

11 Serve avocados in a soup plate surrounded by the curried coconut milk. As the sauce is thin, provide dessert spoons as well as forks to tackle this dish.

WINE

An Alsace Pinot Blanc (white)

INGREDIENTS

2 ripe avocados

juice of half a lemon

25 g/1 oz butter, melted

400 ml/¾ pt tin of coconut milk

1 tsp hot curry paste

FOR MOUSSE

(Cold ingredients help mousse to bind)

110 g/4 oz fresh uncooked fillet of whiting, skinned, boned and chilled

1 cold egg

150 ml/¼ pt cream, chilled

1 tsp dry sherry or dry white wine, chilled

salt and ground white pepper

ground nutmeg

OPTIONS

This basic mousse can also be mixed with 25 g/1 oz of uncooked chopped prawns at step 2 above. Spoon the mixture into ramekins and bake for 15 minutes at 200°C/400°F/gas mark 6 to produce individual whiting and prawn mousses.

If the avocados are too hard, put them in a paper bag in a warm place for a few days to ripen.

Warm Smoked Salmon with Spinach Dressing

4 portions
Oven: 220°C/425°F/gas mark 7

INGREDIENTS

8 slices of smoked salmon
mound of mixed lettuce, shredded

FOR DRESSING
45 g/1 ½ oz fresh spinach leaves
100 ml/3 ½ fl oz sunflower oil
1 ½ tbs balsamic vinegar
½ tsp fresh lemon juice
salt and ground black pepper

METHOD

1 Make equal-sized mounds of lettuce on four starter plates.
2 Drape two smoked salmon slices over each mound.
3 Blend or liquidise together the spinach, oil, vinegar and lemon juice.
4 Season with salt and pepper.
5 Warm each plate of smoked salmon in the hot oven for a minute.
6 Pour the dressing over and around the salmon mounds and serve.

Facing page: Warm Smoked Salmon with Spinach Dressing

Baked Fish Gateau

6 portions/4 generous portions using ramekins with 150 ml/¼ pt capacity
Oven: 200°C/400°F/gas mark 6

♦ A water bath is needed for this dish, i.e., any oven-proof tin/tray which can hold enough hot water to reach halfway up the sides of the ramekins. This helps the dish to cook evenly and keeps the fish moist.

INGREDIENTS

350 g/12 oz mixed fresh fish – uncooked (salmon, white fish, shellfish)

150 ml/¼ pt each of milk and cream

1 tbs fresh fennel or dill, finely chopped

¼ tsp ground nutmeg

salt and ground white pepper

4 eggs

25 g/1 oz butter, melted

METHOD

1 Poach fish in milk and cream with herbs, nutmeg and seasoning for six minutes.

2 Strain and reserve liquid and keep fish separately.

3 Beat strained liquid and eggs together.

4 Brush inside of ramekins with butter and fill each one three-quarters full with fish.

5 Top up with the liquid egg mixture and bake in a water bath for about 25 minutes when the gateaux should be just firm to the touch.

6 Serve hot or cold in or out of the ramekins.

OPTIONS

The spinach sauce (see p 53) served over this hot or cold starter is delicious.

WINE

A French Chardonnay (white)

Mushrooms stuffed with Hummus and Vinaigrette

4 portions
Oven: 190°C/375°F/gas mark 5

12 medium open-cap mushrooms
without stems
4 tbs olive oil
2 tbs fresh lemon juice

FOR HUMMUS

125 g/4 oz dried chickpeas,
soaked for 4 hours
juice of 2 lemons
3 tbs light tahini paste
2 garlic cloves, crushed
salt
1 tbs olive oil

FOR GARNISH

6 tbs parsley, finely chopped
2 tbs paprika
For vinaigrette dressing
1 tbs white wine vinegar
4 tbs sunflower oil
1 tbs sesame oil
salt and ground white pepper

OPTIONS

If you are in a hurry, substitute 2 x
400 g/140 oz can of chickpeas,
drained, for dried chickpeas – these can
be used immediately.

Hummus is also delicious as a snack or
starter with toast, pitta bread or
crudités.

METHOD

1 First make hummus by draining chickpeas and simmering in fresh water until tender – about one hour.

2 Drain and keep the cooking water.

3 Blend the chickpeas, lemon juice, tahini, garlic, salt and oil with a sufficient amount of the cooking water to ensure a soft creamy consistency.

4 Prepare mushrooms by combining 4 tablespoons olive oil and 2 tablespoons lemon juice in a bowl and brushing liberally inside and outside of mushroom caps. Bake for 15 minutes and cool.

5 Spoon hummus into mushroom caps and mould into cone shapes with a moist knife. Coat half the cone with parsley and the other half with paprika for a two-tone effect.

6 Make the vinaigrette dressing by whisking or liquidising vinegar and oils together.

7 Season with salt and pepper and serve separately in a bowl on the table.

8 Arrange the mushrooms on four plates and serve with french bread or soda bread.

9 The vinaigrette can be dipped into, or dribbled over the mushrooms.

Good, wholesome meat and poultry main courses need not be tedious to prepare. The main course recipes included here are biased in favour of quick cooking. I have, however, included two meat dishes – Old-Fashioned Beef Olives and Spiced Pork Roast – which take time to prepare and are slow-cooked, giving them the advantage of intensified flavours and little last-minute work. None of the meat or poultry recipes is very expensive. Some, like Grilled Lamb Kidneys with Lemon and Onion Purée, are positively cheap when you consider the cost per person. Above all I have sought to offer a variety of meat and poultry in these dishes and various methods of cooking them.

Old-Fashioned Beef Olives

♦ Recipes for stuffed beef rolls or olives are to be found in old Irish as well as European cooking. My recipe is an amalgam of various ideas.

METHOD

1 Make stuffing by combining all the stuffing ingredients to a thick paste in a food processor and seasoning with salt and pepper.

2 Next, to prepare the meat, stretch the beef slices by placing them on a chopping board and beating them firmly with a meat mallet or rolling pin for a few seconds. Alternatively, ask your butcher to do this when you buy the meat.

3 Lay the rashers trimmed to size on each beef slice and season.

4 Divide the stuffing equally among the slices of topside. Roll them up and tuck in the ends.

5 At this stage either tie each roll with cotton string lengthwise and crosswise or secure it with a couple of cocktail sticks. This much preparation can be done well in advance of the remaining work.

(Cont'd on following page)

INGREDIENTS

FOR BEEF OLIVES

12 thin slices of topside approx 8 x 10 cm/3 x 4 inch in size

12 rindless back rashers

salt and ground black pepper

1 tbs sunflower oil

1 medium onion, finely chopped

2 medium carrots, chopped in 0.5 cm/¼ inch pieces

1 stick of celery, finely chopped

6 juniper berries, crushed

2 garlic cloves, crushed

1 tbs tomato paste

150 ml/¼ pt dry cider

15 fl oz/¾ pt beef stock

2 bay leaves

1 tbs fresh sage, chopped

FOR STUFFING

50 g/2 oz brown breadcrumbs

1 small onion, grated

zest and juice of half a lemon

50 g/2 oz mushrooms, chopped

2 tsp tomato paste

1 tbs fresh parsley, chopped

2 garlic cloves, crushed

1 egg

1 tbs sunflower oil

salt and ground black pepper

Old-Fashioned Beef Olives

(Cont'd)

6 Heat the oil in a deep heavy-based pan or fireproof casserole and brown the beef olives on all sides.

7 Add onion, carrot, celery, juniper, garlic and tomato paste. Mix and cook gently for four minutes.

8 Add cider and stock, bay leaves and sage. Bring to the boil and simmer covered for an hour and a half, skimming off any fat that gathers on the surface.

9 Remove the beef and keep warm.

10 Strain the stock and reduce quickly in a pot over high heat until it reaches a gravy consistency. Alternatively, if in a hurry, mix a little stock with a teaspoon of cornflour and whisk back into the sauce to thicken. Check the seasoning.

11 Remove string or cocktail sticks from the beef and serve with lots of sauce and Garlic Mashed Potatoes (see p 77).

WINE

A Rhône red

Spiced Pork Roast, Apple and Thyme Cream Sauce

4 portions
Oven: 150°C/300°F/gas mark 2

1 First prepare the stuffing by cooking the onion and garlic in butter until soft.

2 Add the herbs and breadcrumbs.

3 Cool a little before mixing in the egg.

4 Season well with salt and freshly ground pepper.

5 Prepare the meat by trimming off any excess fat and pricking the centre of the meat with a kitchen fork.

6 Combine all the spicy paste ingredients and brush the meat with half this mixture.

7 Spread the stuffing over the meat.

8 Roll the meat up and tie firmly with cotton string.

9 Brown the meat with a little oil in a roasting tin over a hot flame or ring and then roast, seam-side up, for three hours. If using loin, cook for only two hours.

10 Halfway through cooking, remove the joint from the oven and brush liberally with the remaining spicy paste.

11 Return to the oven seam-side down and continue cooking.

12 Meanwhile make the sauce by putting all the ingredients in a pot and bringing to the boil. Simmer for 15 minutes.

13 Discard the thyme.

14 Liquidise the mixture, strain and season to taste. If it seems too thick, adjust the texture with extra stock.

15 Serve the sliced meat on heated plates with liberal amounts of sauce.

WINE

A New World Chardonnay (white)

INGREDIENTS

1 pork belly or loin of pork, about 1.4 kg/3 lb

FOR STUFFING

1 medium onion, finely chopped

3 garlic cloves, crushed

75 g/3 oz butter

bunch of mixed fresh herbs, finely chopped

225 g/8 oz fine breadcrumbs

1 egg, beaten

salt and ground black pepper

FOR SPICY PASTE

2 tbs butter, melted

2 tbs apple chutney

1 tbs fresh lemon juice

2 garlic cloves, crushed

2 tbs 'Lakeshore' Guinness-flavoured mustard

FOR SAUCE

2 large cooking apples, peeled, cored and chopped

1 medium onion, peeled and chopped

2 garlic cloves, crushed

2 sprigs thyme

150 ml/¼ pt chicken stock

½ pt cream

Lamb Cutlets with Honey, Apricot and Tarragon Sauce

4 portions (3 cutlets per person)
Set grill at full

METHOD

1 To make the sauce, soak dried apricots in chicken stock with tarragon for three hours minimum.

2 Blend the soaked apricots, chicken stock, tarragon, honey, lemon juice and seasoning in a food processor until smooth.

3 Heat in pot to just below boiling point.

4 To prepare the meat, mix honey, oil and curry paste together and brush over the cutlets liberally.

5 Season and grill cutlets for three minutes on each side if preferred rare, eight minutes for well done.

6 Arrange cutlets on plate and pour generous amounts of hot sauce over. Serve.

WINE

A Bordeaux or Californian red

INGREDIENTS

FOR CUTLETS

12 lamb cutlets weighing about 900 g/2 lb in total

2 tbs clear honey

1 tsp hot curry paste

2 tbs olive oil

salt and ground black pepper

FOR SAUCE

110 g/4 oz dried apricots

400 ml/¾ pt chicken stock

2 tbs fresh tarragon leaves, chopped

1 tsp clear honey

2 tsp fresh lemon juice

salt and ground black pepper

▶ OPTIONS

This sauce is equally good cold with pâtés, terrines and cold meats.

acing page: Lamb Cutlets with Honey,
pricot and Tarragon Sauce

Grilled Lamb Kidneys with Lemon and Onion Purée

4 portions
Set grill at full

METHOD

1 Make the purée by softening the butter over a medium heat, adding lemon zest, onions, seasoning and mixing well.

2 Cover and stew gently over a very low heat for about 30 minutes until the onions are soft. Cool a little.

3 Purée in a food processor with the lemon juice and season again if necessary. Keep hot or, if the purée has been prepared in advance, reheat.

4 Prepare the meat by peeling the outer membrane off the kidneys and washing well in cold running water. Dry on kitchen paper.

5 Cut each kidney almost, but not quite, in half and cut away the centre core.

6 Toss kidneys in melted butter. Season and grill for two minutes each side if preferred rare, four minutes for well done.

7 Dry kidneys on kitchen paper and serve on a mound of lemon and onion purée.

WINE

A light red, such as a Beaujolais

INGREDIENTS

12 lamb kidneys
25 g/1 oz butter, melted
salt and ground black pepper

FOR PURÉE

50 g/2 oz butter
grated zest of half a lemon
450 g/1 lb onions, finely chopped
salt and ground black pepper
2 tbs fresh lemon juice

▶ OPTIONS

Lemon and onion purée is also delicious with pan-fried liver and sausages.

Baked Chicken Breast with Tagliatelle and Sweet Pepper Sauce

4 portions
Oven: 200°C/400°F/gas mark 6

INGREDIENTS

FOR SAUCE

550 g/1 lb red peppers, seeded and sliced

1 medium onion, sliced

3 tbs olive oil

1 large ripe tomato, chopped

2 garlic cloves, crushed

sprig of thyme

salt and ground black pepper

400 ml/¾ pt chicken or vegetable stock

FOR CHICKEN AND PASTA

½ tbs sunflower oil

4 x 175 g/6 oz chicken breasts, skinned

salt and ground white pepper

50 ml/2 fl oz white wine

150 ml/5 fl oz chicken stock

a bay leaf

225 g/8 oz tagliatelle (for fresh pasta, decrease amounts by half and boil for 3-4 minutes) ◄

OPTIONS ◄

If using fresh tagliatelle, use a lot more water – six times the quantity of pasta. Add a tablespoon of oil, two teaspoons of salt and simmer for about five minutes until al dente. Pasta is cooked when it rises to the surface.

This sauce is equally good with vegetables or fish and will keep in a fridge for several days.

METHOD

1 To make sauce, put peppers, onion and oil in a deep pan and cook slowly, covered, over gentle heat until soft – about 15 minutes.

2 Add tomato, garlic and thyme. Season and add in the stock.

3 Cook for a further 15 minutes, covered.

4 Process or liquidise.

5 Pass through a fine sieve and keep hot until ready to serve.

6 To make chicken and pasta, heat oil in an oven-proof casserole or dish big enough to hold four chicken breasts.

7 Fry chicken for two minutes on each side and season.

8 Add wine, stock and bay leaf. Cover with foil and bake for about 20 minutes.

9 While chicken is cooking, prepare tagliatelle as instructed on packet and keep warm.

10 Remove dish from oven. Take breasts from dish and pat dry on kitchen paper.

11 Carve each breast in two and serve with the pasta and the sweet pepper sauce.

WINE

A Tavel rosé

Facing page: Baked Chicken Breast with Tagliatelle and Sweet Pepper Sauce

Pan-Roasted Barbary Duck Breasts in Sweet Pepper Marmalade

Oven: 200°C/400°F/gas mark 6
4 portions

INGREDIENTS

4 boneless Barbary duck breasts
1 tbs icing sugar
2 tbs ground cinnamon
salt and ground black pepper
150 ml/¼ pt chicken stock

FOR SWEET PEPPER MARMALADE
MAKES 225G/½ LB
1 medium-sized red and yellow pepper
1½ tbs olive oil
1 small onion, finely sliced
1 large garlic clove, crushed
1 tbs white wine vinegar
1 tbs clear honey
seeds from one cardamom pod, crushed
⅛ tsp Tabasco
salt and ground black pepper

OPTIONS

You can double up the quantities for sweet pepper marmalade and store the excess in sterilised jars in the fridge and use as a chutney with cold meats or other savoury dishes.

METHOD

1 Make marmalade by charring and blistering whole peppers under a hot grill.
2 Put peppers in a bowl, cover with a towel and seal by placing a plate on top like a lid. After 10 minutes it should be easy to remove the skins from the peppers. Seed and slice thinly.
3 Heat the olive oil in a pan or pot.
4 Add onion and garlic and cook for one minute.
5 Add all other ingredients except salt and pepper and cook gently for 30 minutes until soft and jammy.
6 Season.
7 Add stock to marmalade and heat.
8 Prepare duck breasts by making four criss-cross slashes on the fat side of each breast with a sharp knife.
9 Put sugar and cinnamon into a shallow dish or tray.
10 Dip and press each breast, skin side, into the sugar and cinnamon.
11 Fry, skin down, in a heavy-based pan for about six minutes over steady, medium heat until the sugar caramelises.
12 Discard three-quarters of the fat that has accumulated and transfer breasts, skin up, to an ovenproof dish. Roast 10 minutes for medium, 15 to 20 minutes for well done.
13 Serve duck breasts on mounds of the liquid marmalade. Store surplus marmalade in sealed jars.

WINE

A Gewürztraminer (white)

Facing page: Pan-Roasted Barbary Duck Breasts in Sweet Pepper Marmalade

Chicken and Ham Dumplings in Chinese Broth

INGREDIENTS

600ml/1 pt Chinese broth (see p 14)

700 g/1½ lb chicken breast, chopped

110 g/4 oz chicken liver
(frozen/defrosted livers can be used)

225 g/8 oz cooked ham, chopped

2 garlic cloves, crushed

1 tsp chilli, minced

1 tbs Chinese oyster sauce

1 tsp Chinese five-spice powder

1 tbs fresh coriander, chopped

3 eggs

150 ml/¼ pt dry white wine

150 ml/¼ pt chicken stock

225 g/8 oz fine breadcrumbs

OPTIONS ◄

Egg noodles would complement this
dish perfectly.

METHOD

1 Heat Chinese broth and keep hot.

2 In a food processor blend all ingredients except breadcrumbs into a smooth paste.

3 In a large bowl combine this mixture with the breadcrumbs and shape with your hands into dumplings the size of golfballs.

4 Poach (boil at a simmer) in the simmering Chinese broth for 10 minutes and serve with broth in wide soup bowls or deep dinner plates.

WINE

A Fumé Blanc (white)

Main Courses

FISH

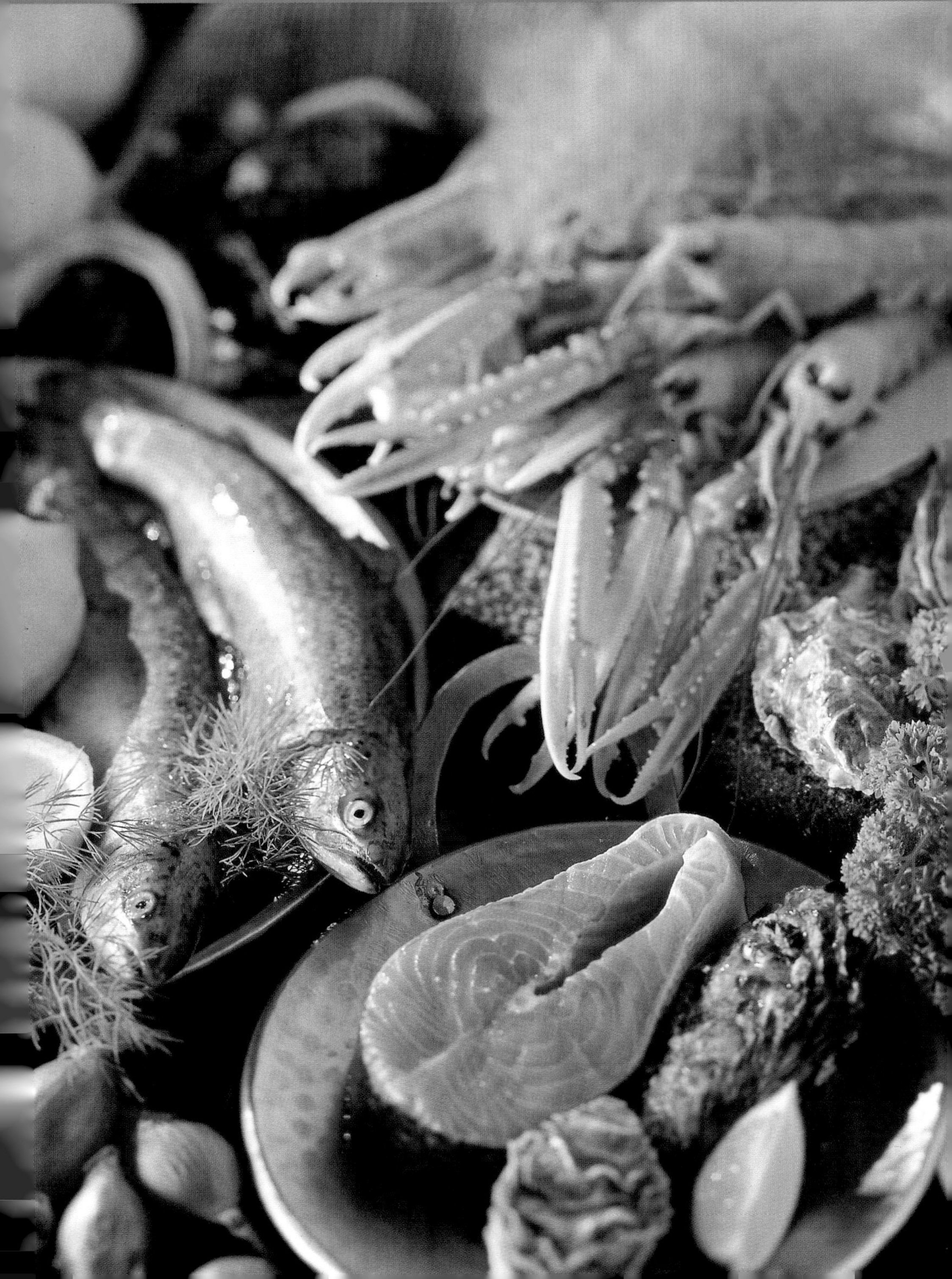

Ray, salmon, monkfish, mussels, prawns – all appear in the following recipes. I have included a lot of different types of fish and shellfish here, but I could have spread the net even wider – I might have added tuna and squid, both now more regularly available. Cooks can include them, if fancied, in the Seafood Couscous.

I could even have gone dangerously exotic with a recipe for fugu, a Pacific fish of great status in Japan. It can kill if not properly prepared. I decided to forego fugu.

Despite increasing levels of pollution in Irish waters, the Atlantic seas are still gloriously rich in fish. Nor have those horrors, the factory ships that resemble battleships, exhausted resources yet. Miraculously, nature survives to provide Ireland with some of the best seafood to be found anywhere.

Fish is a low-fat, healthy food. I have heard one fishmonger proclaim with absolute conviction that eskimos, whose diet is predominantly fish, swim with an ease and virtuosity beyond the scope of mere carnivores. So now!

Poached Fish Sausages in Chive Butter Sauce

4 portions, 2 sausages per person

METHOD

1 Weigh 50 g/2 oz trout fillet separately and chop into very small pieces. Keep chilled.

2 Chop whiting and the rest of the trout roughly and process to a paste in a food processor.

3 Add cream and egg whites gradually.

4 Transfer to a cold, deep bowl and fold in the small pieces of trout and the fennel with a spatula.

5 Season and refrigerate for five minutes.

6 Using eight sheets of clingfilm (20 cm/ 8 inch square), roll the mixture into eight sausages (10 cm/4 inch long x 2 cm/1 inch thick), knotting the clingfilm at either end of each sausage.

7 Poach in simmering, salted water for about 10 minutes until springy to the touch.

8 Nip each clingfilm knot with a scissors and the sausages will slip out easily.

9 Make the sauce by reducing vinegar, wine and shallots over heat to approximately two tablespoons of liquid.

10 Whisk in the cream and bring to the boil.

11 Take the pan off direct heat and whisk in the butter pieces little by little, putting the pan back on a low heat three or four times so that the butter melts. The mixture must not boil.

12 When all the butter has been whisked into the sauce add the lemon juice and seasoning.

13 If you prefer you may strain out the onions.

14 Add the chives just before serving.

15 Serve the sausages hot with chive butter sauce.

WINE

A Sauvignon Blanc (white)

INGREDIENTS

450 g/1 lb fresh trout fillet, well chilled

450 g/1 lb fresh whiting fillet, well chilled

275 ml/½ pt cream, well chilled

2 egg whites, lightly beaten, well chilled

2 tbs fennel or any other anise-flavoured herb such as chervil or sweet cicely, finely chopped

salt and ground white pepper

FOR SAUCE

75 ml/3 fl oz white wine vinegar

75 ml/3 fl oz dry white wine

1 tbs shallot or onion, finely chopped

1 tbs cream

150 g/5 oz cold butter cut into 12 pieces

1 tsp fresh lemon juice

salt and ground white pepper

2 tbs chives, chopped

▶ OPTIONS

Freshly-made sausages can be kept in the fridge for a couple of days or frozen for a month. Halve the quantities to make an excellent starter.

These sausages can be made ahead of time to step 6. They can then be refrigerated for up to two days until needed.

Leftover cooked sausages can be served cold with salad as a starter or snack.

Grilled Salmon with Fruit and Citrus Salsa

4 portions
Set grill to hot

♦ Farmed salmon is now one of the cheapest types of fish and can be very good quality. The wild variety, however, is always superior.

METHOD

1 Make the salsa by gently mixing all the ingredients, seasoning and setting aside, covered, to marinate for an hour.

2 Season and then dip salmon portions in oil and grill, skin side up, for about three minutes until the skin chars.

3 Turn and cook for six or seven minutes. The fish should be just cooked and moist. If undercooked salmon is preferred, test it after about four minutes.

4 Serve, skin side up, on the tart juicy salsa.

WINE

A Chablis (white)

INGREDIENTS

▶**FOR SALSA**

50 g/2 oz ripe fresh pineapple, peeled, cored and chopped in small, even pieces

1 medium dessert apple, peeled, cored and chopped as above

1 ripe mango, peeled, stone removed and chopped as above

4 strawberries, chopped as above

25 g/1 oz cucumber, chopped as above

2 large ripe tomatoes, skinned, seeded and chopped as above

1 small red onion, peeled and chopped finely

1 medium red chilli, seeded and chopped finely

1 tbs dill, chopped finely

juice of 2 limes and 1 orange

salt and ground white pepper

2 tsp sesame oil

FOR THE FISH

4 x 175 g/6 oz salmon fillets, unskinned

1 tbs sunflower oil

salt and ground white pepper

▶ OPTIONS

Salsa goes with any grilled or barbequed fish – tuna, halibut, swordfish, shark.

Monk and Mussel Stir-Fry

4 to 5 portions

450 g/1 lb uncooked monkfish or rock salmon, filleted and trimmed

225 g/½ lb cooked mussels (see below)

4 spring onions, sliced

1 small carrot, sliced thinly

½ celery stick, sliced thinly

6 medium mushrooms, sliced

2 small peppers (1 red, 1 green), seeded and sliced thinly

1 small red chilli, seeded and finely chopped

15 g/½ oz root ginger, finely chopped

2 medium garlic cloves, crushed

25 g/1 oz unsalted peanuts

1 tbs Worcester sauce

1 tbs Chinese oyster sauce

2 tsp grain mustard

2 tsp Chinese five-spice powder

150 ml/¼ pt dry white wine

400 ml/¾ pt fish stock

2 tbs sesame oil

OPTIONS ◀

This is a substantial dish on its own. However, if you wish to serve an accompaniment, rice or noodle are good with it.

METHOD

1 Cut monkfish into 5 cm/2 inch strips and set aside in a bowl with the mussels.

2 Mix together the spring onions, carrot, celery, mushrooms, peppers, chilli, ginger, garlic and peanuts and keep aside in another bowl.

3 Combine all the other ingredients except sesame oil in another bowl.

4 Heat the oil in a large wok or skillet.

5 Add the vegetables and nuts and stir-fry for a minute.

6 Add the monkfish and mussels and stir-fry for another minute.

7 Pour in the spiced liquid. Cover and simmer for about three minutes.

8 Serve in deep plates.

TO COOK MUSSELS

1 Clean and de-beard 225 g/½ lb mussels.

2 Put mussels in a large pot and add a medium onion, finely chopped, and one tablespoon of chopped parsley.

3 Pour in 150 ml/¼ pt dry white wine. Cover and steam over a high heat for about five minutes, shaking the pot a couple of times.

4 The mussels are cooked when the shells open. Discard any that remain closed.

5 Cool a little and remove mussel meat from shells.

WINE

A dry white, such as Macon or Rhone

Previous pages: Monk and Mussel Stir-Fry

Prawns, Baked Potato and Pesto

4 portions
Oven: 200°C/400°F/gas mark 6

METHOD

1 Make the pesto by mixing together in a food processor half the oil and all other pesto ingredients. After 30 seconds gradually add the rest of the oil. Season. Set aside two tablespoons for immediate use – the rest will keep in a sealed jar, refrigerated for at least two weeks.

2 Make a 5 cm/¼ inch incision all around the 'equator' of each potato. Bake for an hour.

3 When cool enough to handle, cut each potato in half lengthwise and hollow out the centre, leaving one-third of the potato attached to the skin. Mash the scooped-out potato with egg yolks and milk. Season and keep on the side in a piping bag.

4 Heat butter in a large pan. Add onion and cook gently for two minutes.

5 Add prawns. Sprinkle with cayenne and toss carefully with butter and onion for a minute. If using frozen prawns, 30 seconds cooking time is sufficient.

6 Remove prawns to a bowl on the side.

7 In the same pan boil the wine until reduced by half. Add the cream and reduce again for about three minutes. Stir in pesto and lemon juice and boil for another minute.

8 Add prawns and cool.

9 Fill the potato shells with the creamy prawns. Pipe mashed potato on top and bake for 12-15 minutes. They should be hot and golden-coloured.

10 Serve two filled potato halves per portion, garnished with basil leaves.

WINE

A Sauvignon Blanc (white)

INGREDIENTS

4 large baking potatoes, unskinned
2 egg yolks
1 tbs milk
salt and ground white pepper
50 g/2 oz butter
50 g/2 oz onion, finely chopped
450 g/1 lb fresh prawns, peeled
pinch of cayenne pepper
150 ml/¼ pt dry white wine
300 ml/½ pt cream
2 tsp fresh lemon juice
basil to garnish

▶FOR PESTO
MAKES 225 G/½ LB

50 g/2 oz Parmesan, grated
50 g/2 oz basil leaves
25 g/1 oz fresh parsley
50 g/2 oz pine nuts
15 g/½ oz walnuts
2 medium garlic cloves, crushed
275 ml/½ pt olive oil
salt and ground black pepper

▶ OPTIONS

Most households will have no difficulty in using up the excess pesto which is addictive with pasta, soups, sauces, sandwiches, meat and fish.

The preparation to step 8 can be done several hours in advance.

If using frozen prawns, defrost thoroughly overnight in fridge and discard any excess liquid.

Seafood Couscous

4 portions

INGREDIENTS

1 tbs sunflower oil

1 medium onion, finely chopped

1 medium carrot, chopped small

2 garlic cloves, crushed

1 medium courgette, sliced

4 medium mushrooms, sliced

1 tbs raisins

6 tbs couscous

1.1 lt/2 pt fish stock

450 g/1 lb mixed fish shellfish, uncooked except mussels (see p 46) white fish and salmon cut into 5 cm/2 inch pieces

juice of 1 lemon

2 tsp ground cumin

1 tsp harissa or chilli sauce (see p 111)

salt and ground white pepper

OPTIONS ◀

This is an attractive dish for an informal dinner party, served with a big salad.

◆ Couscous is a type of hard wheat semolina that has been ground, then moistened and rolled in flour. It is popular in North Africa where it is usually steamed and served with stews, broths or even some sweet dishes. Almost all the couscous available in Ireland is already cooked and needs only the addition of stock or water to be perfectly edible. Like rice, couscous is versatile and a wonderful absorber of flavours.

METHOD

1 Heat oil in a large, heavy-based pan.
2 Fry onion and carrot for two minutes.
3 Add garlic, courgette, mushrooms and raisins and cook for a further three minutes.
4 Add couscous and stir well, cooking for another minute.
5 Add half the stock and cook, covered, over low heat for three minutes more.
6 Mix in the fish. Pour in the rest of the stock and the lemon juice.
7 Incorporate the cumin and harissa/chilli paste using a big spoon to spread the spices well.
8 Cover again and simmer for five minutes.
9 Season and serve.

WINE

A dry Spanish rosé

Facing page: Seafood Couscou

Fried Ray Wing, Capers and Anchovy Dressing

INGREDIENTS

FOR DRESSING

1 x 50 g/2 oz can anchovy fillets in oil

1 garlic clove, crushed

juice of 2 lemons

1 tsp Dijon mustard

3 tbs mayonnaise/crème fraîche

¼ pt fish stock

FOR FISH

4 x 175 g/6 oz ray wing fillets, skinned (total of 700 g/1 ½ lb)

50 g/2 oz butter

salt and ground white pepper

2 oz capers with a little juice

1 tbs parsley, finely chopped

OPTIONS

This versatile dressing can be used for pan-fried dishes, for salads or with less stock as a dip with crudités or a fondue sauce.

METHOD

1 Make the dressing by blending all dressing ingredients in a food processor or liquidiser.

2 Two pans may be required to cook the ray wings. Alternatively fry in two batches keeping the fried fish hot while the next batch cooks. If using two pans heat half the butter in each and fry ray wings for about four minutes each side. Season with salt and pepper and transfer fish to plates.

3 Toss the capers in an empty pan for a few seconds and then scatter them over the fish portions.

4 Dribble the dressing liberally over the ray and sprinkle them with chopped parsley before serving.

WINE

A Pouilly Fuissé (white)

Cooking vegetarian dishes is both a challenge and a liberation because it is territory largely unexplored, ripe for discovery. I have been interested in it for many years and we feature full vegetarian menus in Drimcong where it is heartening to note that demand is increasing. Diners who are not vegetarian at all will now happily try a vegetarian course. Conservative carnivores should allow themselves to have an occasional vegetarian dish, they might even live longer – playwright George Bernard Shaw, a dedicated vegetarian, survived into his nineties! I have little medical knowledge and I am no expert in dieting. However, I can say that it is vital that a vegetarian diet should be planned carefully. The best way to ensure a strictly vegetarian diet is balanced is to combine a variety of foods from each of the five main food groups:

1 The milk group – all kinds of cheeses, yoghurt and dishes rich in milk, such as soups, sauces, milk and cream-based desserts;

2 The meat substitute group – fish, tofu, nuts and seeds, cheese again, peas, beans, lentils, eggs;

3 Fruit and vegetables – fresh green and root vegetables, canned, frozen and dried vegetables, fresh, canned and dried fruits, seaweeds like carrageen and dillisk;

4 Cereals and potatoes;

5 Fats and sugars in moderation.

Anybody embarking on strict vegetarian eating should consult a nutritionist.

Ricotta and Walnut Dumplings with Spinach Sauce

6 portions
Have a large pan of boiled, salted water and a bowl of iced water ready

METHOD

1. Drain the ricotta cheese well.
2. Mix with egg and season well.
3. Add walnuts and two-thirds of the grated hard cheese and mix in the flour a third at a time. The mixture should be soft and dry.
4. Turn this dough onto a floured worktop and divide into two.
5. Roll into two long sausages about 2.5 cm/1 inch thick and then cut into 2 cm/¾ inch lengths. Simmer in the boiling salted water until the dumplings float – about two minutes.
6. Immerse cooked dumplings in the bowl of iced water for two minutes and then spread them out singly on a cloth-covered tray.
7. Cover with another damp cloth.
8. To make the sauce, heat half the oil and butter in a pan and cook the onions for a minute.
9. Add garlic and cook for a further minute.
10. Add wine and reduce briskly by half.
11. Add cream and stock and reduce again by half – about two minutes over high heat.
12. Add spinach and basil and simmer for a minute.
13. Place in processor and liquidise until smooth. Keep warm.
14. Heat remaining oil and butter in a non-stick pan and fry dumplings on both sides until golden.
15. Remove from the pan. Sprinkle with the remaining cheese and brown briefly under a hot grill.
16. Serve with the sauce.

INGREDIENTS

450 g/1 lb ricotta cheese

1 egg

salt and ground black pepper

50 g/2 oz walnuts, toasted and well chopped

50 g/2 oz grated hard cheese such as Parmesan or regato

50 g/2 oz plain flour

FOR SAUCE

2 tbs sunflower oil

45 g/1 ½ oz butter

50 g/2 oz onion, finely chopped

1 large garlic clove, crushed

100 ml/3 ½ fl oz dry white wine

200 ml/7 fl oz cream

200 ml/7 fl oz vegetable stock

50 g/2 oz fresh spinach, chopped

2 tbs fresh basil, chopped

This recipe is an adaptation of a popular vegetarian starter by chef Anton Edelman at London's Savoy Hotel.

WINE

A Chianti (red)

Sweetcorn Pancakes with Crème Fraîche, Apple and Raspberry Sauce

4 starters/2 main courses/4 desserts

♦ Yes, this is a triple-purpose recipe! It is sufficiently savoury to be a starter or main course and, with increased sugar, makes an unusual dessert.

INGREDIENTS

BATTER FOR FOUR THICK PANCAKES

1 x 340 g/12 oz can sweetcorn kernels, drained

50 ml/2 fl oz milk

2 eggs

1 tbs sunflower oil (keep an extra 2 tbs in a small jug to fry the pancakes)

50 g/2 oz plain white flour

½ tsp salt and a pinch of white pepper

FOR FILLING

225 g/8 oz crème fraîche

1 large dessert apple such as a Granny Smith, peeled, cored and chopped

2 tsp fresh lemon juice

1 tbs cream

1 tsp sugar if making starter or main course pancakes; 3 tsp sugar if making dessert pancakes

salt and white pepper

FOR RASPBERRY SAUCE

225 g/8 oz raspberries

25 g/1 oz icing sugar

1 tsp fresh lemon juice

METHOD

1 Make the batter in a food processor by blending the sweetcorn, milk, eggs and one tablespoon oil together for a minute.

2 Gradually add the flour with the processor speed reduced to safeguard against spatters and spills.

3 Pour batter into a jug, season and stir.

4 Brush a 19 cm/7½ inch non-stick frying pan with a little of the reserved oil and stand over high heat for a minute.

5 Turn down the heat a little, pour in a quarter of the batter and cook for about three minutes each side. Keep warm and continue with the next pancake and so on.

6 Make the filling by combining all ingredients together in a bowl. Season.

7 Make the raspberry sauce now by liquidising the sauce ingredients and straining through a sieve fine enough to exclude the raspberry seeds. You can call it a 'coulis' if you want to flaunt your culinary French!

8 Divide the filling equally between pancakes. Fold each one into a half-moon shape and pour the raspberry sauce over. Serve.

WINE

A Beaujolais (red)

Spaghetti with Vegetables and Pesto

4 portions

METHOD

1 In a large pot bring 4 litres/7 pints of water to a fast boil.

2 Add salt, spaghetti and vegetables.

3 Cook until the pasta is al dente – about five minutes. It should be cooked but still have a bite. When the pasta is cooked, so are the vegetables.

4 Drain in a colander and retain about two tablespoons of the cooking water. Transfer pasta and vegetables to a hot serving dish.

5 Stir the retained water into the pesto and mix and toss with the pasta and vegetables.

6 Serve with a bowl of grated parmesan or regato cheese.

WINE

A New Zealand Chardonnay (white)

INGREDIENTS

1 ½ tbs salt

▶ 400 g/14 oz spaghetti

50 g/2 oz French beans, finely chopped

50 g/2 oz baby sweetcorn, finely chopped

50 g/2 oz red pepper, finely chopped

50 g/2 oz courgettes, finely chopped

4 tbs pesto (see p 47)

4 tbs grated Parmesan or regato cheese

▶ Seek out good dried pasta made from 100 percent durum-wheat flour. Very often so-called 'fresh pasta' is badly made and therefore does not cook well – the axiom 'fresh is best' does not necessarily apply to pasta. It is important to remember also that once pasta is cooked and tossed in its sauce it should be served immediately.

Chickpea Cakes with Goat's Cheese and Tomato Salsa

4 portions
Grill at hot

INGREDIENTS

½ slice brown or
white loaf bread, toasted

1 x 425 g/15 oz can chickpeas, drained

1 tbs grated regato or other hard cheese

1 tbs fresh coriander, finely chopped

1 tbs parsley, finely chopped

1 tsp harissa (see p 111) or chilli sauce

1 tsp fresh lemon juice

1 small garlic clove, crushed

1 egg

salt and ground white pepper

1 tbs sunflower oil

225 g/8 oz goat's cheese

FOR TOMATO SALSA
MAKES 400 ML/¾ PT

6 medium tomatoes, skinned, seeded
and chopped

4 spring onions, finely sliced

2 small garlic cloves, crushed

1 tbs fresh mint, finely chopped

½ red chilli, finely chopped

150 ml/¼ pt olive oil

1 tbs red wine vinegar

salt and ground black pepper

OPTIONS

This salsa can be used as a salad dressing, with barbequed food, steak or fish. It can be made a day or two in advance and stored in the fridge. If using dried chickpeas soak for four hours and simmer in fresh water for about one hour. Drain and proceed with the recipe from step 1 above.

METHOD

1 In a food processor make crumbs of the toast and gradually add all other ingredients except oil, goat's cheese and tomato salsa.

2 Transfer the processed mixture to a large bowl and mould into four cakes each weighing about 50 g/2 oz and 7.5 cm/3 inch wide.

3 Heat oil in a pan and fry gently for three minutes each side. Transfer to a grilling tray.

4 Mould goat's cheese into 4 x 50 g/2 oz cakes and place on top of the chickpea cakes.

5 To make salsa, mix all ingredients and check seasoning.

6 Spoon a tablespoon of the salsa over each of the goat's cheese cakes and grill until well heated – about three minutes.

7 Serve immediately with a small salad and a bowl of salsa.

WINE

A light Italian red, such as Bardolino or Valpolicella

Facing page: Chickpea Cakes with Goat's Cheese and Tomato Salsa

Carrot and Nut Terrine with Tahini Sauce

4 to 6 portions
Oven: 200*C/400*F/gas mark 6

INGREDIENTS

1 tbs sunflower oil
225 g/8 oz cashew nuts, well chopped
450 g/1 lb carrot, grated
1 medium onion, finely chopped
1 stick celery, finely chopped
75 g/3 oz soft brown breadcrumbs
1 tbs mixed fresh herbs, finely chopped
salt and ground black pepper

FOR TAHINI SAUCE
4 tbs tahini paste
1 garlic clove, crushed
juice of a lemon
150 ml/5 fl oz water
150 ml/5 fl oz natural yoghurt
salt and ground white pepper

♦ Tahini is an oily paste ground from sesame seeds. It has a strong, nutty flavour and is sold in two varieties, light and dark. The latter is stronger and sweeter. Either one is suitable for this recipe, depending on personal taste!

METHOD

1 Heat oil.
2 Fry nuts, carrot, onion, celery and herbs in the oil for five minutes, seasoning and mixing well. Stir and mix in breadcrumbs.
3 Pack the mixture into a greased loaf tin and bake in the oven for 20 minutes.
4 Make tahini sauce by blending all ingredients except salt and pepper in a food processor. Season.
5 Take terrine out of oven, cool, and turn out on a chopping board.
6 Slice into portions. Reheat in the oven and serve with tahini sauce.

WINE

A German Riesling (white)

Rice Balls with Pepper Compôte

4 portions
Set deep fryer at hot or half-fill a deep saucepan with 700 ml/1 pt vegetable oil and heat until a grain of rice sizzles the second it touches it.

METHOD

1 To make the compôte, cook all compôte ingredients in a heavy-based saucepan, covered, for three minutes.

2 Uncover and simmer for 10 minutes. Stir now and then and season to taste. Keep hot.

3 Cook the rice as if you were making a risotto: in a large pan sauté the shallot or onion and garlic in the vegetable oil and butter.

4 As they begin to colour add the finely chopped dried apricots, the spices and the rice.

5 Stir until all the grains of rice are coated, and then little by little, add the boiling stock, only adding more as the stock becomes absorbed in the rice.

6 The risotto should be just sticky – not too liquid. Season with salt and pepper. Allow to cool.

7 Form the rice into golfball-sized balls with floured hands.

8 Deep-fry until just crispy. Drain and serve on the Pepper Compôte.

WINE

A Spanish Rioja (red)

INGREDIENTS

FOR PEPPER COMPÔTE

1 red, 1 yellow and 1 green pepper, seeded and sliced thinly

2 medium onions, sliced thinly

1 tbs olive oil

1 tbs white wine

1 tbs clear honey

1 tbs white wine vinegar

salt and ground white pepper

FOR RICE

1 tbs vegetable oil

25 g/1 oz butter

1 shallot or small onion, finely chopped

1 garlic clove, chopped

40 g/1½ oz mixed dried apricots, finely diced

1 tsp ground coriander

1 tsp ground cumin

pinch of ground ginger

176 g/6 oz arborio rice or pudding rice

1 lt/1¾ pt vegetable stock

salt and ground white pepper

50 g/2 oz plain white flour, for coating fingers

Couscous with Vegetables, Nuts and Dried Fruit

4 portions

1 tbs sunflower oil

1 medium onion, finely chopped

2 medium carrots, chopped small

3 garlic cloves, crushed

2 medium courgettes, sliced

2 tbs mixed nuts

1 green and 1 red pepper, seeded and sliced

6 mushrooms, sliced

2 tbs raisins

1 tbs dried figs, chopped

2 tbs dried apricot, chopped

6 tbs couscous

2 pt vegetable stock

2 tbs fresh lemon juice

2 tsp harissa (see p 111) or chilli paste

2 tsp ground cumin

salt and ground black pepper

METHOD

1. Heat oil in a large heavy-based pan.
2. Fry onion and carrot for two minutes.
3. Add garlic, courgettes, nuts, peppers, mushrooms and fruit and fry for a further three minutes, mixing well.
4. Add couscous and combine with the other ingredients.
5. Add stock and cook covered for three minutes.
6. Mix in lemon juice, harissa/chilli paste and cumin and simmer for another two minutes, covered. Serve as is or with salad.

WINE

An Australian Shiraz (red)

OPTIONS ◄

Left-over, cold couscous is a lovely salad on its own or with the addition of chopped herbs, spring onions and tomato, oil and vinegar.

SALADS

Salads are serious business these days – good for us, and full of the vitamins for healthy living. Our anti-salad culture is beginning to accept the sound health reasons for an increasing intake of fresh vegetables. Slowly, inevitably, the strong arguments are bearing fruit, as it were. There is, however, another valid reason for salad days – they bring out the creativity and frivolity in cooks. One can build colourful domes and castles of crisp lettuces, exotic fruit, frilly fronds of fennel, all massaged and glistening with herb vinegars and aromatic oils. Food for the sensual as well as the serious!

The Simplest
Salad

4-6 portions,
depending on size of lettuce heads

METHOD

1 Wash lettuce and discard wilted leaves.
2 Separate leaves and toss in a large salad bowl.
3 Add herbs and toss again.
4 Whisk together the lemon juice, olive oil and sugar. Season and whisk again.
5 Season the salad. Pour on the dressing and toss again.
6 Serve immediately.

INGREDIENTS

2 fresh heads of lettuce of choice
2 tbs fresh herbs, chopped
1 tbs fresh lemon juice
4 tbs olive oil
1 tsp sugar
salt and ground black pepper

► OPTIONS

If you are tempted to complicate this salad add a few chopped cherry tomatoes, radishes and spring onions.

SALADS   63

Pink Grapefruit, Avocado and Fennel Salad

4 portions

♦ A lovely light salad, attractive to look at and fresh-tasting. It has the extra advantage of producing its own dressing.

INGREDIENTS ◄

2 pink grapefruit, peeled and segmented, juice retained

2 ripe avocados, peeled and cut in 1 cm/½ inch pieces

175 g/6 oz fennel bulb, cut in 1 cm/½ inch pieces or same amount of white cabbage, shredded

1 tbs sesame oil

salt and ground black pepper

4 iceberg lettuce 'shells' (when an iceberg lettuce is cut in two, shell-shaped leaves can be picked off either half)

4 fennel sprigs

OPTIONS ◄

If pink grapefruit are unavailable use ordinary grapefruit and add four tablespoons of orange juice to supplement the dressing.

METHOD

1 In a bowl make the dressing by mixing the grapefruit juice and sesame oil.

2 Season.

3 Place an iceberg 'shell' on each of four plates and sprinkle with a little grapefruit and sesame dressing.

4 Spoon equal quantities of grapefruit, avocado and fennel into each lettuce 'shell' and pour more dressing on top.

5 Garnish with fennel sprigs.

Facing page: Pink Grapefruit, Avocado and Fennel Sala

Tomato and Onion Salad in Balsamic and Hazelnut Dressing

4 portions
Oven: 200°C/400°F/gas mark 6

INGREDIENTS

10 medium ripe tomatoes
2 medium onions, very finely chopped
2 tbs hazelnuts
4 tbs olive oil
1 tbs balsamic vinegar
1 tsp fresh lemon juice
1 garlic clove, crushed
salt and ground black pepper
2 tbs chives, chopped

METHOD

1 Slice tomatoes thinly and arrange in a salad bowl with chopped onion sprinkled on top.

2 Roast hazelnuts for a few minutes until golden. Take out of the oven and rub off skins with a dry cloth. Grind thoroughly in a food processor.

3 Make the dressing by whisking or shaking together the oil, vinegar, lemon juice and garlic. Season.

4 Add chopped chives and ground hazelnuts to the dressing, whisk again and pour over the tomatoes and onion.

OPTIONS ◄

This salad is especially good in late summer when the new season's tomatoes are in their prime. Try it with smoked salmon and brown bread!

Tabouleh

♦ Couscous is very versatile – here it is used in a salad which is particularly associated with summer when fresh mint is abundant, and I can think of no better complement to barbecued meat or fish.

METHOD

1 Soak couscous, just covered, in cold water for 20 minutes and drain off excess water, if any.

2 In a bowl, mix couscous with lemon juice and season.

3 Add the oil, parsley, mint, spring onion and tomato, combining gently but thoroughly.

4 Serve in a large bowl so that everyone can help themselves.

INGREDIENTS

225 g/8 oz couscous

water to cover

juice of 2 lemons

salt and ground black pepper

3 tbs olive oil

1 tbs fresh parsley, finely chopped

3 tbs fresh mint, finely chopped

6 spring onions, finely sliced

4 medium tomatoes, skinned, seeded and chopped

Radish and Dill Salad, Yoghurt and Orange Dressing

4 portions

INGREDIENTS

24 medium-sized radishes
salt and ground black pepper
4 tbs natural yoghurt
1 tbs horseradish sauce
juice of 1 fresh orange
2 tbs dill, finely chopped
4 sprigs of dill to garnish

METHOD

1 Slice radishes. Season well and arrange on four salad plates.
2 Make the dressing by mixing together yoghurt, horseradish sauce, orange juice and chopped dill.
3 Pour dressing over radishes and garnish with sprigs of dill.

OPTIONS ◀

Sharp and fresh tasting, this salad could also serve as a light first course. To turn it into a substantial summer lunch it could be teamed up with Tomato and Onion Salad (see p 66)

(see p 66)

Facing page: Radish and Dill Salad Yoghurt and Orange Dressing

Boilíe Cheese with Pickled Carrot and Toasted Pine Nuts

4 portions

INGREDIENTS

FOR PICKLED CARROTS

6 medium carrots, peeled and grated

1 tbs fresh lemon balm or mint, chopped

700 ml/1 pt vegetable stock

150 ml/¼ pt white wine vinegar

700 ml/1 pt orange juice

1 tsp white granulated sugar

salt and ground white pepper

FOR CHEESE AND DRESSING

2 x 200 g/7 oz jars Boilíe cheese

3 tbs black olives, chopped

1 garlic clove, crushed

1 medium red onion, finely chopped

½ medium red chilli, finely chopped

2 tsp white wine vinegar

salt and ground white pepper

3 tbs pine nuts, toasted, to garnish

METHOD

1 Make the pickle by first mixing carrot and lemon balm or mint in a deep bowl.

2 In a pot bring to the boil the stock, vinegar, orange juice and sugar and boil for a minute.

3 Pour mixture over the carrot and lemon balm.

4 Mix and season.

5 Set aside to cool.

6 Drain the Boilíe cheese through a sieve and reserve the oil.

7 Mix the drained oil with the olives, garlic, red onion, chilli and two teaspoons vinegar to make a dressing. Season.

8 Divide the pickled carrots between four plates with no more than a tablespoon of pickling juice each.

9 Place Boilíe cheese balls on top of the carrot.

10 Mix the dressing well and dribble on and around the cheese.

11 Just before serving toast the pine nuts and sprinkle over each portion.

OPTIONS

Other cheese possibilities include feta, with two teaspoons per person of olive oil added. Boilíe is one of the great examples of modern Irish cheesemaking. Not surprisingly it won gold status at the London International Cheese and Dairy Competition in 1997. Boilíe is available in two types: cow's and goat's. Either, or a combination of both, may be used in the above recipe.

Vegetables

The six vegetable dishes included in this section are purposely varied. I have also tried to give recipes using vegetables that might be considered less 'sexy' than the ubiquitous broccoli. Turnip and cabbage remind us, I suppose, of poorer times when Irish cuisine was not as sophisticated as it is today. However, both turnip and cabbage have several advantages over other vegetables – they are still cheap, native to Ireland and available for long periods throughout the year. Carrot is another undervalued vegetable while the cherry tomato inclusion is, I suppose, a nod in the direction of modernity. These fragrant little fruits are so delicious, particularly the organic variety, that I can't resist including them here. And the potato dishes? Well, it's back to our roots again. Mashed potato has been an Irish staple for centuries – as has the potato cake which I have dressed in new clothes by matching it with carrot and parsnip.

Carrot Mousse

4 portions
Oven: 200°C/400°F/gas mark 6

Use ramekins with 150 ml/¼ pt capacity.
You will need a water bath (see p 23).

METHOD

1 Put carrots, half the butter, sugar, cinnamon and orange zest in a pot and just cover with water.
2 Bring to the boil and continue boiling until the liquid has evaporated and carrots are tender.
3 Liquidise carrots together with hot cream.
4 Season and cool for a few minutes.
5 Add egg and yolks and liquidise again.
6 Brush four ramekins with the remaining butter and fill with the purée.
7 Bake in a water bath for about 30 minutes until set.
8 Remove from the oven. Rest for 10 minutes and turn out of ramekins.
9 Sprinkle with parsley. Serve with chicken, fish or lamb or as a vegetarian starter with pesto (see p 47).

INGREDIENTS

4 medium carrots, peeled and thinly sliced

1 tbs melted butter

1 tsp granulated white sugar

pinch of cinnamon

grated zest of 1 washed orange

a little water

275 ml/½ pt cream, heated

1 whole egg plus 3 egg yolks

salt and ground white pepper

Turnip Bake

INGREDIENTS

4 garlic cloves, crushed

1 large onion, finely chopped

250 ml/8 fl oz milk

300 ml/12 fl oz cream

1 ½ tsp nutmeg, grated

1 tbs sunflower oil

1 large Swede turnip, peeled, quartered and very thinly sliced

salt and ground black pepper

OPTIONS ◄

Turnip Bake goes particularly well with roasts – turkey, pork, duck, goose. Keep it in mind for Christmas Day when it makes a nice alternative to Brussels sprouts. It also improves with age – any extras can be reheated and used next day or frozen for later use.

METHOD

1 In a pot add garlic and onion to milk, cream and nutmeg and bring to the boil. Take off heat and leave to infuse.

2 Brush a deep, oven-proof baking dish all over with the oil and build layers of the turnip slices, seasoning each layer as you go along.

3 Pour the infused liquid, including garlic and onions, evenly over the turnip and bake for about 1 ½ hours.

4 Every 20 minutes press the turnip firmly with an egg slice. This helps in the process of compacting the bake and absorbing the liquid. If the top of the bake begins to brown before the turnip is completely cooked, cover it with foil and continue baking.

5 Serve immediately or refrigerate for later use.

Facing page: Turnip Bak

Sautéed Cherry Tomatoes with Parsley and Thyme

4 portions

INGREDIENTS

700 g/1 ½ lb cherry tomatoes
2 garlic cloves, crushed
4 tbs fresh parsley, finely chopped
1 tbs fresh thyme, finely chopped
75 ml/3 fl oz olive oil
2 tsp sugar
salt and ground black pepper

OPTIONS ◄

Anybody who likes tomatoes will be happy to serve this simple dish with any main course.

METHOD

1 Rinse and dry tomatoes thoroughly with kitchen paper.
2 Remove stems.
3 Mix together the garlic, parsley and thyme.
4 Using a wok or large pan heat the oil until it begins to move on the surface.
5 Add the tomatoes.
6 Sprinkle with sugar and season well.
7 Add the garlic/parsley/thyme mixture and toss gently until the herbs soften – about two minutes. The tomatoes should give to the touch but not split open.
8 Serve in a hot dish.

Garlic Mashed Potatoes

4 portions

METHOD

1 Put potatoes in a saucepan with milk and garlic.
2 Add enough water to just cover potatoes.
3 Bring to the boil. Cover and simmer for about 20 minutes until potatoes are cooked.
4 Drain potatoes and keep 150 ml/¼ pint of the liquid, discarding the rest.
5 Return potatoes to the saucepan and mash with cream and butter until lump-free. If necessary some of the reserved liquid can be used to moisten the mash.
6 Season and serve.

INGREDIENTS

550 g/1 ½ lb potatoes, peeled and cut into 1 cm/½ inch chunks

50 ml/2 fl oz milk

4 large garlic cloves, crushed

a little water

50 ml/2 fl oz cream

50 g/2 oz soft butter

salt and ground white pepper

► OPTIONS

Garlic Mash is perfect with Old-Fashioned Beef Olives (see p 27) and it would also be suitable with Poached Fish Sausages (see p 41) and virtually any children's dinner.

Stir-Fried Cabbage with Mushroom, Onion and Bacon

4 portions

INGREDIENTS

1 tbs sunflower oil
1 tbs sesame oil
1 small onion, finely chopped
6 button mushrooms, finely sliced
4 streaky rashers, very thinly sliced ◄
450 g/1 lb cabbage, shredded
salt and ground black pepper

METHOD

1 Heat oils in a large deep pan or wok.
2 Stir-fry onion, mushrooms and rashers for two minutes.
3 Add cabbage and stir-fry for a further three or four minutes.
4 Season and serve.

OPTIONS ◄

Stir-fried cabbage will set off all kinds of main courses, whether meat or fish.

Vegetarians may omit the bacon.

Facing page: Stir-Fried Cabbage with Mushroom, Onion and Bacon

Potato and Vegetable Cake

4 portions

INGREDIENTS

500 g/1 lb large potatoes in their skins

4 medium carrots, peeled

3 medium parsnips, peeled

½ tsp salt and ground black pepper

50 g/2 oz sunflower oil

OPTIONS ◄

There are many variations to this cake such as:

1 Fried bacon and onion bits can be introduced to the grated vegetables and potato before cooking.

2 For an interesting pizza-style finish, spread tomato salsa (see p 56) and grated cheese on top and heat under a hot grill for a few minutes.

METHOD

1 Boil the potatoes in a saucepan for 10 minutes and drain well. Cool for two minutes.

2 Peel the still-hot potatoes and let them cool for a few more minutes.

3 Grate the potatoes, carrot and parsnip coarsely into a large bowl.

4 Season and mix well with salt and pepper.

5 Heat half the oil in a large non-stick frying pan. Add the grated potato and vegetables and flatten to a cake shape.

6 Fry for about 10 minutes over medium heat until well browned underneath.

7 Turn carefully, add the remaining oil and cook again until well browned – about six to seven minutes.

8 The cake should now slide easily onto a serving plate. Cut into wedges and serve.

Desserts, sweets, puddings! What should we call them? I have always had difficulty with 'pudding'. It is inadequate because it excludes so much. One could hardly call 'peaches and cream' a pudding. My idea of a pudding is of something cooked, hot and very often savoury, as in Yorkshire pudding. The very word 'pudding' conjures up for me visions of posh ladies in restaurants demanding imperiously of young waiting staff: 'What's for pudding?' 'Sweet' is more acceptable. At least it gets the message across. Like pudding, however, sweet is limited. Not all 'sweets' are literally sweet. Is it correct to describe a fruit salad as sweet? I am happier with dessert. It sounds inclusive, an umbrella word for ice creams, chocolate concoctions, pastries, pancakes, fresh fruit.

Despite my prejudice, there is a pudding in this dessert selection! There is also an emphasis on fresh fruit, particularly fresh local fruit in season.

Apple and Lemon Sorbet

METHOD

1 In a saucepan, over a gentle heat, combine all ingredients until sugar dissolves and apples soften – about 15 minutes.

2 Pass through a sieve and cool for 30 minutes.

3 Process to a thick firm consistency in an ice cream machine if you have one. Otherwise put the cooled apple mixture in a container in the coldest part of the freezer and whisk vigorously at hourly intervals until frozen – five to six hours. The result will not be as smooth as with the machine method but it will, of course, taste just as good.

WINE

An Italian sparkling white, such as Asti Spumante

INGREDIENTS

6 medium Granny Smith apples, peeled, cored and chopped

150 ml/¼ pt fresh lemon juice

150 ml/¼ pt apple juice

50 g/2 oz castor sugar

► OPTIONS

This light, refreshing sorbet would be an appropriate end to any heavy dinner. Sorbets such as this, which are not too sweet, can also double as palate cleansers between courses. Alcohol fans might like a tablespoon or two of cider or apple brandy poured over it. It would team up nicely with Hot Pineapple Pudding instead of the Ginger Custard Sauce (see p 89).

Cassata Ice

900 g/2 lb loaf tin
About 8 portions

♦ My version of this Italian ice cream is close to the original. It differs in that I use an ordinary loaf tin rather than an oval mould and I substitute dry sherry for marsala, a very sweet, fortified wine, which I think is too sweet for the cassata.

INGREDIENTS

5 eggs separated, keep only 3 egg whites, 5 egg yolks

75 g/3 oz castor sugar

400 ml/¾ pt cream

8 glacé cherries, chopped

25 g/1 oz good quality dark chocolate, grated

190 g/6½ oz fruit and nut mix

50 ml/2 fl oz dry sherry

METHOD

1 Line loaf tin with clingfilm.
2 Beat egg yolks and 2 oz of the sugar until creamy.
3 Whip cream to Irish Coffee thickness and fold into egg yolks and sugar.
4 Gently incorporate the cherries, chocolate, fruit and nut mix and sherry.
5 Beat the three egg whites, gradually adding the remaining 1 oz sugar until stiff.
6 Fold stiff egg whites into the larger mixture. Combine well and pour into the loaf tin.
7 Freeze.
8 Once frozen the cassata will slip easily out of the tin. Do remember to peel away the clingfilm before slicing into portions.

OPTIONS ◄

The cassata can be prepared in individual moulds or ramekins and, if not all used at one sitting, can be stored in the freezer for a few weeks.

WINE

A Muscat de Beaumes de Venise (white)

Dessert Pizza

6 pizzas, 12 cm/5 inch diameter
Oven: 200°C/400°F/gas mark 6

1 Make pizza bases by sieving flour and icing sugar into a mixing bowl.

2 Add butter and mix to a breadcrumb texture.

3 Combine egg yolk.

4 Remove from mixing bowl and knead to a smooth dough.

5 Cover and chill for an hour.

6 Roll out to a 0.5 cm/¼ inch thickness.

7 Cut out pizza circles to 12 cm/5 inch diameter and bake for about 15 minutes until golden and crisp.

8 Cool and place in the centre of six serving plates.

9 Make topping by liquidising or processing the raspberries or strawberries and pass through a fine sieve.

10 Spread a tablespoon of fruit purée over each pizza to within 2.5 cm/1 inch of the edge.

11 Spread cream or crème fraîche gently over purée.

12 Arrange mixed fruit on top of cream.

13 Sprinkle a tablespoon of grated chocolate over each pizza.

14 Decorate with chopped mint.

WINE

A Vouvray sparkling white or any medium dry sparkling white wine

INGREDIENTS

FOR SHORTBREAD BASE

125 g/4½ oz plain white flour

40 g/1½ oz icing sugar

90 g/3½ oz soft butter

1 egg yolk

FOR TOPPING

225 g/8 oz raspberries or strawberries, liquidised, which produces
150 ml/¼ pt purée

150 ml/¼ pt thick whipped cream or crème fraîche

450 g/1 lb mixed fresh fruit (I use a mixture of sliced strawberry, apple, grape and orange segments)

6 tbs good quality dark chocolate, grated

6 tsp fresh mint, finely chopped

Pancakes

12 pancakes using a 20.5 cm/8 inch non-stick pan

METHOD

1 Blend the flour, butter, milk and salt to a smooth batter.

2 Heat the pan with a little oil.

3 Make thin pancakes one after the other ensuring that the pan is hot and lightly oiled each time before you pour in the batter.

4 Sprinkle each finished pancake with castor sugar and cool before stacking one on top of the other.

5 Serve simply with lemon juice and more sugar.

INGREDIENTS

3 eggs

100 g/3 ½ oz plain white flour, sieved

50 g/2 oz butter, melted

275 ml/10 fl oz milk

pinch of salt

1 tsp, or to taste, of castor sugar per pancake

1 tsp vegetable oil per pancake

3 lemons, quartered, to serve

▶ OPTIONS

If storing pancakes for later use put a disc of greaseproof paper between each one to avoid sticking. They can then be frozen.

These pancakes are delicious served with ice cream, Banana and Honey Sauce or Sugar Syrup (see p 88)

Banana and Honey Sauce

6-8 portions

1 tbs clear honey

225 g/10 oz ripe bananas, peeled

juice of 1 lemon

275 ml/10 fl oz sugar syrup

½ tsp ground ginger

FOR SUGAR SYRUP

110 g/4 oz castor sugar

275 ml/½ pt water

few drops fresh lemon juice

1 Warm honey by sitting the honey jar in hot water.

2 Slice bananas and toss in lemon juice.

3 Make sugar syrup by dissolving sugar and water in a saucepan over gentle heat.

4 Add lemon juice and boil for a minute.

5 In a saucepan bring sugar syrup, ginger and honey to the boil. Add bananas and simmer for five minutes.

6 Liquidise for a minute and pass through a wire-mesh sieve into a bowl.

7 Stir for a minute. Allow to cool and refrigerate until ready to use.

8 Serve hot or cold with pancakes, ice cream, fruit tarts, fruit salad or crumbles.

An Asti Spumante, Italian sparkling white

Hot Pineapple Pudding with Ginger Custard Sauce

4 portions
Oven: 200°C/400°F/gas mark 6

Use ramekins with 150 ml/¼ pt capacity

METHOD

1 Make the Ginger Custard Sauce by boiling the milk with the ginger. Take off the heat.

2 Whisk egg yolks together in a large bowl until thick and pale. Add in the hot milk and ginger and mix well.

3 In a clean pot reheat the custard, stirring gently until the sauce is thick enough to coat the back of a spoon. Do not boil.

4 Cool and allow the ginger to infuse for an hour.

5 Brush the insides of the ramekin dishes with the melted butter. Next, prepare the pudding by heating the golden syrup a little and stir in the ground ginger.

6 Pour syrup and ginger into the ramekins – a teaspoon per dish.

7 Trim the pineapple and cut into four circular discs to fit neatly into the base of each ramekin. Chop the pineapple trimmings and keep separately.

8 Beat together butter and sugar in a bowl until light and fluffy. Mix in the eggs.

9 Mix chopped pineapple trimmings with flour and baking powder and fold into the beaten butter/sugar/egg mix.

10 Divide this mixture between each ramekin. Level off the tops and bake for **20-25 minutes.**

11 Cool slightly and turn out.

12 Strain the sauce and reheat without boiling.

13 Serve poured over the hot pudding.

WINE

A Côteaux de Layon (white)

INGREDIENTS

1 tbs butter, melted to grease ramekins

4 tsp golden syrup

½ tsp ground ginger

► ½ fresh pineapple, peeled and cored

110 g/4 oz soft butter

110 g/4 oz castor sugar

4 eggs

110 g/4 oz plain flour, sieved

½ tsp baking powder

FOR GINGER CUSTARD SAUCE

¾ pt milk

25 g/1 oz fresh root ginger, finely chopped

6 egg yolks

50 g/2 oz castor sugar

► ## OPTIONS

Canned pineapple rings, strained of juice, can be used instead of fresh pineapple.

Hot Chocolate Soufflé in Sabayon Sauce

4 portions
Oven: 220°C/425°F/gas mark 7

Use ramekins with 150 ml/¼ pt capacity

INGREDIENTS

150 g/5 oz good quality dark chocolate, broken in small pieces

2 tbs soft butter

3 eggs, separated

3 tbs castor sugar

FOR SABAYON SAUCE

2 egg yolks

2 tbs castor sugar

90 ml/3½ fl oz of medium dry white wine

½ tbs fresh lemon juice

OPTIONS

Believe it or not, it is possible to cook and keep soufflés in advance. As they cool the soufflés will deflate – you can then turn them out of the ramekins and refrigerate. When you are ready to serve, reheat them in a hot oven for a few minutes and serve with the sabayon sauce. they will not be as light and puffed as the soufflés straight from the oven but they will still be presentable.

The sabayon can be made into a cold sauce after step 2 by placing the bowl over ice or iced water and whisking until cold, then folding in three tablespoons of lightly whipped cream.

The Italians call sabayon sauce 'zabaglione' and serve it in glasses with sponge fingers. It is sweet, light and alcoholic, and can be served as a dessert on its own. It is also delicious with Christmas pud.

♦ The most important thing to say about this recipe is that it is not difficult. Don't be intimidated by the fearsome reputation of soufflés.

METHOD

1 Melt chocolate and half the butter in a heavy-based saucepan over a very low heat.

2 Remove from heat and pour into a large, deep bowl, using a plastic spatula.

3 Whisk egg whites to stiff peaks, gradually adding the sugar.

4 Combine egg yolks with the chocolate/butter mix.

5 Using a metal spoon, stir a quarter of the stiff egg whites into the chocolate/butter mix and fold in the rest. This much preparation can be done in advance if desired and the mixture refrigerated until needed.

6 Brush ramekins with the remaining butter and fill three-quarters full with the soufflé mixture.

7 Bake for about 20 minutes until well risen.

8 Meanwhile, make the sauce by putting all Sabayon ingredients in a bowl over a pot of simmering water. (The water should not touch the base of the bowl.)

9 While sauce is simmering, whisk it by hand or with a hand-held electric whisk until the Sabayon is thick and fluffy and much increased in volume.

10 Serve immediately as a sauce with hot chocolate soufflés.

WINE

A French Sauternes (white)

Facing page: Hot Chocolate Soufflé in Sabayon Sauce

Strawberry Gratin

Set grill at hot
4 portions

INGREDIENTS

450 g/1 lb fresh strawberries
hot sabayon sauce (see p 90)

OPTIONS

Choose this dessert in June and July when local strawberries are at their freshest. Any other fresh fruit or combination of fruits is suitable for this treatment.

METHOD

1 Wash, pick off stems and dry strawberries.
2 Divide the fruit equally between four grill-proof plates.
3 Pour the prepared sabayon sauce over strawberries and grill until golden brown. Watch closely, as the browning happens quickly.
4 Serve immediately.

WINE

A New World sweet white wine, such as a Riesling

BREADS AND BAKING

Baking is great therapy. Not only is it a basic and simple activity, but it has the added advantage of giving satisfying results without the ministry of an expensive psychiatrist – just hands, worktop and dough. Serious bakers are a breed apart and I am in awe of them. They are invariably blessed with good sense and an unmistakable other-worldliness. Is it their prolonged association with yeast that lends them this elevated air? Bakers know secrets of life that I never will. They know about sunrise, milkmen, somnambulists, early mists and the sounds that are drowned out by day. And they know all about the power of smell and aroma. A town or suburb without the smell of a good bakery is less than complete. You can't make up for it at home but you sure can try!

Smoked Salmon Scones

About 15 scones
Oven: 190*C/375*F/gas mark 5

METHOD

1. Mix together smoked salmon, spring onions and lemon zest.
2. In a separate bowl, sieve the flour and baking powder and rub in the butter to make a breadcrumb texture.
3. Fold in the salmon mixture.
4. Add the two eggs to the milk/cream. Mix and beat lightly.
5. Then pour into salmon and flour and mix to a soft dough.
6. Roll out the dough on a clean worktop to a thickness of 2 cm/1 inch and cut into 4 cm/2 inch round scones.
7. Brush scones with egg wash and bake until golden – about 15 minutes.
8. Turn out on to a wire tray to cool.

INGREDIENTS

225 g/8 oz smoked salmon, sliced in small thin pieces

3 spring onions, finely sliced

zest of 1 washed lemon, finely grated

250 g/9 oz plain white flour

2 tsp baking powder

30 g/1 ¼ oz butter

2 eggs, lightly beaten

150 ml/¼ pt half milk, half cream

egg wash: 1 egg and 1 tbs milk, well beaten

▶ OPTIONS

Serve these scones warmed with fish starters or soups.

Toasted, they make a novel breakfast bread with scrambled or fried eggs.

Carrot and Dillisk Bread

1 x 900 g/2 lb loaf
Oven: 140°C/275°F/gas mark 1

◆ This is primarily a savoury bread but it has an element of sweetness in it that makes it acceptable as a tea bread. The use of the seaweed dillisk or dulse lends an unusual and definite taste of the sea.

INGREDIENTS

25 g/1 oz dried dillisk, soaked for 5 minutes in water

110 g/4 oz butter, melted

1 large carrot, grated

4 eggs

50 g/2 oz castor sugar

pinch of salt

250 g/9 oz plain white flour

1 ½ tsp baking powder

METHOD

1 Drain dillisk. Pat dry with a kitchen towel and chop finely.

2 Brush the insides of a loaf tin all over with a little butter.

3 In a mixing bowl combine remaining butter, carrot, eggs, sugar, dillisk and salt.

4 Fold in sieved flour and baking powder.

5 Fill the tin with cake mixture and bake for 40-50 minutes – a skewer inserted in the cake should come out clean.

6 Cool before turning out and slicing.

Facing page: Carrot and Dillisk Brea

Marie's Brown Soda Bread

For a 23 cm/9 inch wide cake
Oven: 200°C/400°F/gas mark 6

♦ This is an old recipe given to my wife, Marie Deering, by her mother. The sunflower seeds are a recent embellishment.

METHOD

1 In a large bowl mix together the two flours, sugar, salt and bread soda.
2 Rub in the butter with your fingers until the mixture resembles fine breadcrumbs.
3 Make a centre 'well' and pour in buttermilk or sour milk.
4 Mix again and shape into a round cake.
5 Sprinkle with sunflower seeds.
6 Bake for 35-40 minutes.
7 Test by inserting a long wooden skewer into the centre of the bread. If it comes out clean the bread is cooked. If tapped on the bottom, it should sound hollow.
8 Take out and cool on a wire tray.

INGREDIENTS

425 g/15 oz wholemeal flour

150 g/5 oz plain white flour

2 tsp sugar

1 tsp salt

1 tsp bread soda

75 g/3 oz soft butter

275 ml/½ pt buttermilk or sour milk (add a tablespoon of natural yoghurt per ½ pint of milk and leave overnight to sour)

25 g/1 oz sunflower seeds

Chocolate Fruit Cake

Makes 2 x 900 g/2 lb loaf tins
Oven: 100°C/200°F/gas mark ½

INGREDIENTS

375 g/13 oz sultanas

225 g/8 oz glacé cherries, halved

225 g/8 oz dried apricots, chopped

175 g/6 oz butter

310 g/11 oz good quality dark chocolate, broken in small pieces

175 g/6 oz light or dark brown sugar

4 tbs brandy

1 tbs sunflower oil

4 eggs, slightly beaten

450 g/1 lb plain white flour

½ tsp bread soda

OPTIONS ◄

This cake will keep for several weeks in the fridge or in an airtight tin. It can also be frozen.

METHOD

1 In a large saucepan over low heat mix together the fruit, butter, chocolate, sugar and brandy. Stir without boiling until well mixed and the chocolate is melted.

2 Boil and then simmer for 10 minutes.

3 Remove from saucepan to a large bowl to cool.

4 Brush the insides of the loaf tins with oil and line with baking parchment or greaseproof paper.

5 Now add and combine eggs with the chocolate fruit mixture, followed by the flour and bread soda.

6 Divide this mixture between the two loaf tins and bake for 1¾-2 hours. The finished cake should be firm yet moist.

7 Cool before removing from tins.

ONE-POT DISHES

One-pot cooking is a guaranteed way to capture the full flavour of ingredients. With all the ingredients enclosed in a pot or casserole there is an interaction and blending of textures and tastes that is unique to this method of cooking. All the goodness of the food is retained and, once served, the liberated aromas are sufficient to activate even the most tired of taste buds.

Both the Boiled Chicken with Vegetables and Pasta and the Burgundy Venison are nutritious and excellent for family dinners, as well as being straightforward to prepare and still tasty when reheated. They are also perfect, cold-weather, comfort recipes, whereas the Chickpea and Sausage Hot-Pot and the Pork and Vegetable Stir-Fry are delicious all year round.

Pork and Vegetable Stir-Fry

4 portions

♦ This one-pot dish takes about 30 minutes advance preparation and about 10 minutes to finish.

METHOD

1 In a bowl toss pork and ginger and set aside.

2 In another bowl mix together vegetables, garlic and peanuts.

3 In a third bowl mix all other ingredients except the sesame oil, salt and pepper and set that aside.

4 Heat the oil in a wok or large, deep pan.

5 When it smokes add pork and ginger and stir-fry for a minute.

6 Add vegetables, garlic and peanuts and stir-fry for three minutes.

7 Add the contents of the third bowl, mix well, cover and simmer for three minutes.

8 Taste, add pepper and salt if necessary.

9 Serve on its own or with a simple salad or rice.

WINE

A Semillon (white)

INGREDIENTS

▶ 700 g/1 ½ lb pork fillet, cut into 5 cm/2 inch strips

25 g/1 oz fresh root ginger, sliced thinly

1 medium carrot, sliced into thin rounds

1 stick celery, sliced thinly

8 medium mushrooms, sliced, any variety

1 medium red pepper, seeded and sliced thinly

2 garlic cloves, crushed

50 g/2 oz unsalted peanuts

1 tbs Worcester sauce

1 tbs light soy sauce

2 tsp grain mustard

2 tsp Chinese five-spice powder

1 tsp minced chilli or chilli sauce

150 ml/¼ pt dry white wine

300 ml/½ pt chicken or vegetable stock

3 tbs sesame oil

salt and ground black pepper

▶ OPTIONS

If you prefer you can substitute chicken for pork.

Chickpea and Sausage Hot-Pot

4 portions

INGREDIENTS

2 tbs olive oil

275 g/10 oz garlic or spicy herb pork sausage, cut in 2.5 cm/1 inch pieces

1 medium onion, finely chopped

1 x 425 g/15 oz can chickpeas

1 x 400 g/14 oz can tomatoes

150 ml/¼ pt chicken or vegetable stock

salt and ground black pepper

2 tbs fresh parsley, finely chopped

fresh brown bread to serve

OPTIONS

If you choose to use dried chickpeas for the hot-pot, follow the soaking and cooking directions outlined in Options on p 56.

METHOD

1 Heat oil in a deep frying pan or saucepan.

2 Fry sausages in pan over medium heat for three minutes.

3 Add onion and continue frying for a further three minutes, tossing and shaking the sausages and onion as you fry.

4 Add chickpeas, tomatoes and stock. Season.

5 Bring to the boil and simmer, covered, for 10 minutes.

6 Stir in the parsley and serve in deep soup plates along with brown bread and butter.

WINE

A Beaujolais or a another light red

Facing page: Chickpea and Sausage Hot-Po

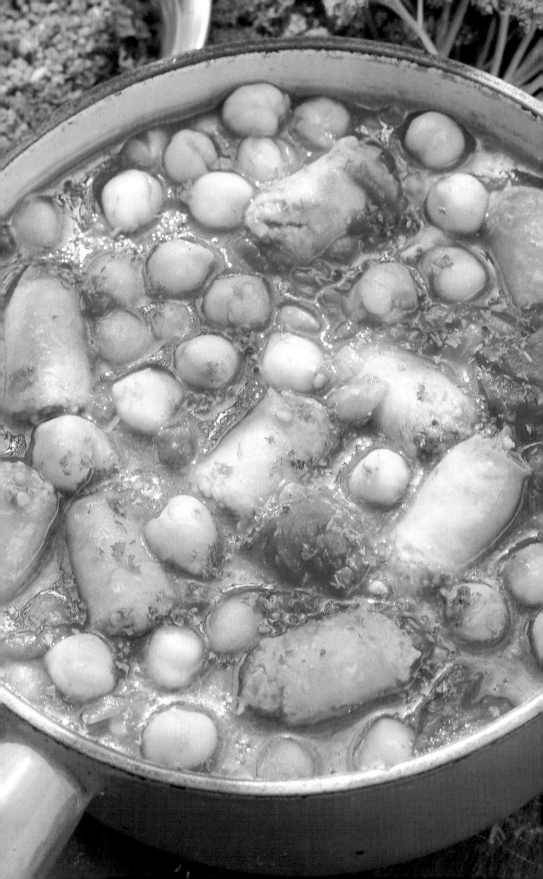

Burgundy Venison

4 portions

♦ Venison is low in fat, a healthy lean meat. Look out for Irish venison which is especially good.

INGREDIENTS

3 tbs sunflower oil

8 thin slices streaky rashers

2 medium onions, thinly sliced

900 g/2 lb stewing venison, cut in 5 cm/2 inch pieces and patted dry with a kitchen towel

2 tbs plain white flour

700 ml/1 pt red wine

700ml/1 pt beef stock

3 garlic cloves, crushed

grated zest of 1 washed orange

6 juniper berries, crushed

bouquet garni ◄

salt and ground black pepper

12 large mushrooms, sliced

2 tbs fresh parsley, finely chopped

OPTIONS ◄

Bouquet garni is the collective French term for herbs to flavour soups, stocks and stews. If you want to make up your own bouquet enclose a bay leaf, a few sprigs of thyme and parsley and lovage in a 'packet' of green leek and secure with string or a cocktail stick. It is also possible to buy a commercially-prepared bouquet garni that looks like a tea bag.

METHOD

1 Heat the oil in a heavy-based pot or deep casserole dish.

2 Brown the rashers in the hot oil and, when crisp, remove and set aside.

3 Fry the onions for about five minutes until brown, add the venison and cook for a further two minutes, turning the meat once so that it too is browned.

4 Sprinkle the meat and onions with flour, stirring until well mixed – about two minutes.

5 Add wine, stock, garlic, orange zest and juniper berries and stir again.

6 Let the liquids boil as you stir and then reduce to a simmer.

7 Add the bouquet garni and season.

8 Cover and simmer for 1½ hours. If the sauce becomes too thick add extra stock.

9 Add bacon and mushrooms, simmer again with the lid off for 20 minutes more. Discard the bouquet garni.

10 Serve with Garlic Mashed Potato (see p 77) or Potato and Vegetable Cake (see p 80) and garnish with parsley.

WINE

A Burgundy (red)

Facing page: Burgundy Veniso

Boiled Chicken with Vegetables and Pasta

4 portions

INGREDIENTS

¼ kg/3 lb chicken, skinned for low-fat version

2 leeks, trimmed and chopped

4 medium carrots, peeled and chopped

2 sticks celery, chopped

2 medium onions, chopped

3 garlic cloves, chopped

water to cover

10 fl oz/½ pt dry white wine

bouquet garni (see note on p 106)

1 chicken stock cube

4 large potatoes, peeled and cut into 8 pieces each

3 oz dried pasta (vermicelli, tagliatelle or spaghetti)

salt and ground white pepper

METHOD

1 Put whole chicken in pot.

2 Add vegetables and garlic and just cover with water.

3 Add wine and bouquet garni and bring to the boil.

4 Crumble in the stock cube and simmer, covered, for 30 minutes.

5 Add potatoes and pasta.

6 Season and simmer, covered, for a further 30 minutes.

7 Lift chicken with a large fork and drain over the pot before placing on a chopping board and dividing into portions.

8 In a deep plate serve each person half a leg and half a breast with lots of vegetables, pasta and broth.

OPTIONS

Having given four people ample portions there should be enough vegetable and pasta broth left for the next day's soup.

WINE

A New World Chardonnay (white)

Accompaniments are a cook's friend in times of need. I turn to them when I'm perplexed about which new flavour or emphasis is called for in a dish. So here are some of my steadfast friends: tapenade for a touch of the Mediterranean; harissa to fire me in the direction of North Africa and its great diversity of spices; chilled butters that bind and mould tastes, preserving flavours that are only liberated when the butters melt over fish, meat or vegetables.

Like good friends, these accompaniments, or cook's companions, stand by until called upon. Take tomato sauce for example – pasta would be bereft without it. And I would feel emasculated if my cupboard didn't contain a jar or two of chutney – that macho preserve that gives soul to a curry.

A word of caution, however: Choose your accompaniments with care. Like a circle of friends they should be picked for their different attributes. They should always be available, but not always needed and certainly not all at the same time!

Harissa

♦ Harissa is a common condiment in North African cooking. It is a spicy sauce, usually hot, sometimes fiercely so, depending on the chillies used. In this recipe I use red chillies which are not too hot – each one is between 10-15 cm (4-6 inches) long.

METHOD

1 Chop chillies roughly and blend to a paste in a food processor with tomatoes, tomato paste, garlic, coriander, cumin and half the vinegar and oil – this should take about a minute.

2 Add the rest of the vinegar, oil and the salt and blend again until the harissa is smooth.

3 Store in a glass bowl or jar, cover with clingfilm and refrigerate.

INGREDIENTS

► 4 fresh red chillies, with stem, seeds and membrane removed

4 medium tomatoes, skinned and seeded

3 tbs tomato paste

3 garlic cloves, crushed

½ tsp ground coriander

1 tsp ground cumin

1 tbs red wine vinegar

2 tbs olive oil

1 tsp salt

► OPTIONS

Harissa prepared this way will keep for at least two weeks in the fridge. It can be used as flavouring for soups, mayonnaise and sauces. Stir a little extra into a tomato salsa to lend more piquancy or into rice, pasta, couscous, curries, mashed potato. Spread a little on top of grilled fish and reheat for a minute.

A few warning notes on chillies!

As a rule, green chillies are usually hotter than red ones and smaller chillies are hotter than larger ones. If you use the seeds in harissa they will make it hotter. When adding chillies to any dish do so in tiny quantities to begin with. Taste and adjust as you see fit. Always wash your hands after preparing chillies.

Tapenade

INGREDIENTS

150 g/5 oz black olives, stoned

1 x 50 g/2 oz tin anchovies, drained

50 g/2 oz capers

2 garlic cloves, crushed

775 ml/3 fl oz olive oil

2 tsp fresh lemon juice

ground black pepper

♦ Nothing symbolises the current popularity of Mediterranean cuisine as well as tapenade. With sun-dried tomatoes, feta cheese and olive oil it has captivated culinary imaginations. I recall making tapenade in our Kinsale restaurant days – a trendy French cookbook of the late 1970s had discovered it. We served it as an accompaniment to sirloin of beef. Nobody liked it. Kinder customers said nothing and scraped it to the side of their plates. One indignant diner exclaimed: 'That black muck is poison!'

OPTIONS ◄ METHOD

Tapenade can be used just like harissa in the various ways listed on p 111. Pair it with sliced tomatoes on a thick slice of french bread or toast as a quick snack or starter. Spread it sparingly on slices of smoked salmon. Then roll the salmon like a cigar and serve as an appetiser with wedges of lemon and brown bread.

1 Put olives, anchovies, capers and garlic in a food processor and blend for a minute.

2 With the machine still on, add oil and lemon juice and blend for another minute.

3 Season with pepper. Pack into a jar and seal with lid or clingfilm. Refrigerate for up to a week.

Facing page: Tapenade

Tuna Mayonnaise

Makes 1 pt, pouring consistency

INGREDIENTS

2 eggs

1 can x 200 g/7 oz tuna in oil

1 garlic clove, crushed

1 tsp Dijon mustard

1 tbs fresh parsley, finely chopped

2 tbs fresh lemon juice

275 ml/½ pt sunflower oil

ground white pepper

OPTIONS ◄

I use tuna mayonnaise with cold fish and hors d'oeuvre. Dribbled over a thick soup it looks like a piece of instant modern art!
Serve it also with chicken and pasta.

♦ This is adapted from an Italian recipe where it accompanied a veal dish.

METHOD

1 Put eggs, tuna (including its oil), garlic, mustard, parsley and lemon juice into a food processor and blend for a minute.

2 With the machine still running add the sunflower oil gradually and continue to process until the mayonnaise is smooth.

3 Season with pepper. It should not need salt as the tuna itself is salty.

4 Keep covered and refrigerated and it will stay fresh for up to 10 days.

Anchovy Butter

Makes about 200 g/7 oz

METHOD

1 Chop anchovy fillets roughly.
2 Combine all ingredients except pepper in a food processor for a minute.
3 Season with pepper and process again for another minute.
4 Using clingfilm, roll into one or two sausage shapes. Refrigerate or freeze.
5 To use, unwrap and slice as required.

INGREDIENTS

50 g/2 oz anchovy fillets in oil
150 g/5 oz soft butter
1 tbs fresh parsley, finely chopped
juice of half a lemon
ground black pepper

▶ OPTIONS

Anchovy butter can be used to intensify fish flavour in sauce or soups: whisk in a little just before serving. It can also be used in other ways such as melting a 1 cm/½ inch slice of the butter over grilled fish, a cooked sirloin steak or a fillet steak. In addition, you can toss cooked vegetables in anchovy butter for extra taste and gloss.

Barbecue Butter

Makes about 225 g/8 oz

METHOD

1 This butter is best mixed with a wooden spoon or spatula. Gradually add all ingredients except salt and pepper to the butter, mixing all the time.
2 Season.
3 Refrigerate and use within three/four days of making. Soften before use.

INGREDIENTS

175 g/6 oz soft butter
1 tbs fresh herbs (a mixture of thyme, mint, sage, parsley), finely chopped
1 tbs tomato ketchup
1 tsp harissa (see p 111) or chilli paste
1 tbs balsamic vinegar
salt and ground black pepper

▶ OPTIONS

This is wonderful brushed liberally over barbecued meat, fish, vegetables.

Mushroom Butter

Makes about 275 g/10 oz

INGREDIENTS

110 g/4 oz mushrooms of any variety
175 g/6 oz soft butter
2 medium garlic cloves, crushed
juice of half a lemon
salt and ground black pepper

OPTIONS ◄

Mushroom butter, like anchovy butter and barbeque butter, is versatile and can be used in similar ways. Additional uses for all three butters will come to mind the more they are used. I tend to use mushroom butter in a wide range of ways and with many different foods, such as spread on savoury biscuits or french bread; piped attractively onto toasted cocktail canapés; tossed and mixed with cooked pasta.

METHOD

1 Slice mushrooms and heat in a pan with 25 g/1 oz butter and the garlic.
2 Simmer for four/five minutes until all juices evaporate.
3 Cool a little and process or mix with the rest of the butter and lemon juice and season.
4 Using clingfilm, roll into one or two sausage shapes. Refrigerate or freeze.

Savoury Breadcrumbs

Makes about 275 g/10 oz

INGREDIENTS

225 g/8 oz fine breadcrumbs
3 tbs fresh parsley, finely chopped
2 tsp sage or thyme, finely chopped
3 garlic cloves, crushed
salt and ground black pepper

OPTIONS ◄

Sprinkle these breadcrumbs liberally over cooked vegetables and potatoes, or grilled or fried fish. Mix them with a little melted butter, and use to stuff tomatoes or mushrooms, or, bound with a beaten egg, as a stuffing for poultry. Try them as a thickening agent whisked into soup

METHOD

1 Toss crumbs, parsley, sage or thyme, garlic and seasoning together until completely and evenly mixed.

Marie's Marmalade

Makes about 6.75 kg/15 lb

♦ In the hierarchy of marmalades this could be described as coarse-cut and bitter-sweet. Stored in a cool, dark place it lasts indefinitely. Our annual supply of 150 lb, made in February, lasts until the next batch is made a year later.

METHOD

1 Put oranges and lemon in a very large pot. Cover with water.

2 Bring to the boil and simmer for two hours.

3 Cool and retain water.

4 Taking oranges and the lemon one at a time, cut in quarters and scoop out pips with a spoon and gather them into makeshift bags made of muslin or unused J-cloths. Tie the bags and keep aside.

5 Blend oranges and the lemon to a pulp in a food processor and weigh the pulp.

6 For every 450 g/1 lb pulp you should have 900 g/2 lbs sugar and 150 ml/¼ pt of the retained water.

7 Mix pulp, sugar and water together. Add the bags of pips and fast boil for 20 minutes.

8 Add 15 g/½ oz butter which helps to prevent scum and continue boiling for another five minutes.

9 Test the consistency of the marmalade by putting a teaspoon of it on a cold plate and letting it sit in the fridge for two minutes. If it wrinkles to the touch it is set. If not, boil again for five minutes and then test again.

10 Using a jug, pour while hot into sterilised jars as for tomato and fruit chutney (see p 122).

INGREDIENTS

2.3 kg/5 lb Seville marmalade oranges, washed – usually available mid-January to mid-February

1 large lemon, washed

water

granulated white sugar

► OPTIONS

Apart from its use as a breakfast preserve, marmalade can be turned into a dessert sauce with the addition of sugar syrup (see p 88) and liquidised or combined with sponge pudding mixture to make orange pudding. A little marmalade whisked with cream produces a lovely bitter-sweet whipped cream.

Onion Marmalade

Makes about 450 g/1 lb

2 tbs olive oil
5 medium onions, finely sliced
1 tbs Grenadine syrup or clear honey
3 tbs red wine vinegar
1 bottle red wine
salt and ground black pepper

Can be served hot or cold and with fish, meat, poultry or game. Its sweet and sour taste goes especially well with game and pork. It can be refrigerated and stored in jars for at least two weeks.

1 Heat the oil in a deep pot or pan.
2 Add onions and toss them in the oil for a minute.
3 Add all other ingredients and bring to the boil.
4 Simmer until most of the liquid has evaporated, stirring and mixing now and then. Season. The marmalade should have a jammy consistency and be a shiny purple colour. This process will take about half an hour.
5 Pack in jars following directions for tomato and fruit chutney (see p 122).

Facing page: Onion Marmalade

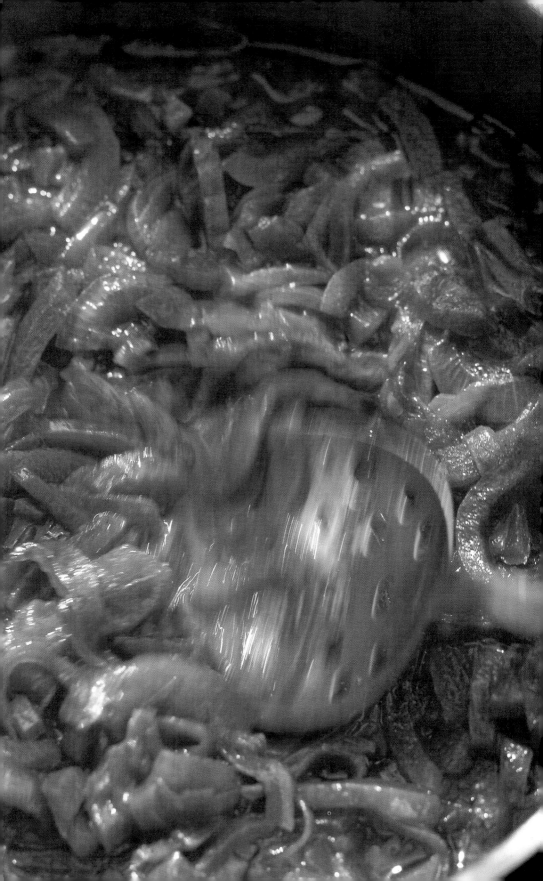

Tomato Sauce

Makes about 400 ml/¾ pt

INGREDIENTS

2 tbs olive oil

450 g/1 lb ripe tomatoes, chopped

1 medium onion, chopped

2 garlic cloves, crushed

1 tbs tomato paste

1 bay leaf

150 ml/¼ pt chicken or vegetable stock

salt and ground black pepper

OPTIONS ◄

Tomato sauce is best made when tomatoes are in season in late summer. Once cooled it can be frozen in small amounts. With the addition of more stock this sauce becomes a soup.

METHOD

1 Heat the oil in a heavy-based saucepan. Add tomatoes, onion, garlic, tomato paste and bay leaf. Stir and cook gently for five minutes.

2 Cover with stock, bring to the boil and then simmer, covered for 15 minutes.

3 Liquidise and strain.

4 Season.

Facing page: Tomato Sauce

Tomato and Fruit Chutney

Makes 1.8 kg/4 lb
Oven: 170°C/325°F/gas mark 3

20 medium tomatoes, peeled, seeded and chopped

450 g/1 lb dried apricots, chopped

110 g/4 oz sultanas

2 large cooking apples, peeled, cored and chopped

2 large onions, finely chopped

150 g/5 oz granulated sugar

700 ml/1 pt cider vinegar

2 tsp ground ginger

½ tsp ground cinnamon

½ tsp ground cloves

salt and ground black pepper

METHOD

1 Combine all ingredients in a large heavy-based saucepan.

2 Bring to the boil and simmer for about two hours by which time the chutney should be thick and most of the liquid evaporated. Season and keep hot.

3 Sterilise glass jam jars by washing in very hot, soapy water and rinsing well. Then place jars on a tray or in a deep roasting tin and heat in the oven for 15 minutes.

4 Pack hot chutney into hot jars and cool.

5 Seal, using jampot covers and store in a cool dry place to mature over two months at least.

OPTIONS ◄

Chutneys, these sweet and sour preserves, go marvellously with all kinds of cooked meats, curries and salads. Stir some into mayonnaise, add a little to gravy or fish sauces and liquidise with a little stock to produce a smooth sauce.

Drimcong Favourites – well, this section should be self explanatory. The choice, however, was not easy. The truth is that my favourites – apart from a few to which I am ever-loyal – are forever changing, and those detailed here are my current crop, plus a couple of long-runners. Ratatouille has been with us at Drimcong for years, although nowadays it features on the menu as part of a mixed hors d'oeuvre. I have been conducting an affair of sorts with black pudding for several years and this recipe, coupling it with white pudding and apple, is easy to prepare. Our hot favourite at the moment is Fish Grill. I love the flexibility it affords – you can use any variety of fish, and sauces or toppings can vary according to resources. It is a good feeling to have a few favourite dishes as a basic repertoire to work with – the more you get to know them the more confident you become.

Ratatouille

4-6 portions for 900 g/2 lb

METHOD

1 Heat oil in a large saucepan.
2 Add onion and garlic and cook for a minute.
3 Add everything else except salt and pepper.
4 Cook, stirring, over medium heat for three minutes.
5 Season, cover and continue cooking gently for 30 minutes, checking and stirring occasionally.
6 If the ratatouille is inclined to dry up, moisten with a little stock or tomato juice or combination of both.

♦ Another intriguing dimension to ratatouille is to turn it into a chutney as follows:

1 In a heavy-based large saucepan, bring 50 g/2 oz sugar to the boil with two tablespoons harissa (see p 111) and 150 ml/¼ pt red wine vinegar, stirring to dissolve the sugar.
2 Add the ratatouille, made according to the recipe above, and simmer uncovered for 20 minutes, stirring now and then.
3 Pack in sterilised jars while still hot as per instructions for tomato and fruit chutney (see p 122).

WINE

A southern French red, such as Fitou

INGREDIENTS

4 tbs olive oil

1 large onion, chopped small

3 garlic cloves, crushed

1 medium aubergine, halved and sliced thinly

3 small courgettes, sliced thinly

1 red and 1 green sweet pepper, seeded and sliced thinly

275 g/10 oz tomatoes, peeled, seeded and chopped

1 bay leaf

1 tbs tomato paste

salt and ground black pepper

► OPTIONS

This Provençale vegetable stew is the most versatile vegetable dish I know. It can be served hot or cold, on its own or as an accompaniment to fish and meat. Vegetarians love it alone and mixed with couscous or rice. It makes an unusual cold starter moulded in ramekins, refrigerated, turned out onto a serving plate and topped with a spoonful of natural yoghurt.

Drimcong Fish Grill

4 portions
Set grill at hot

♦ Here's a dish that uses many of the recipes we love at Drimcong.

INGREDIENTS

2 tbs sunflower oil

225 g/8 oz salmon, cut in 4 equal pieces

225 g/8 oz cod, cut in 4 equal pieces

225 g/8 oz mackerel, cut in 4 equal pieces

50 g/2 oz mushroom butter (see p 116)

50 g/2 oz tapenade (see p 112)

50 g/2 oz tomato salsa (see p 56) mixed with 1 tsp of harissa (see p 111) or chilli sauce

4 large oysters opened, top half shell discarded and oysters resting in the bottom half

50 g/2 oz pesto (see p 47)

OPTIONS

This is currently the most popular fish dish in Drimcong. We vary the fish according to availability. Toppings, too, can vary to include different butters, ratatouille, perhaps, with the oysters, chutney as a topping, savoury crumbs as a topping. Do watch the second phase grilling carefully. Some toppings brown more quickly than others and may burn if left too long under the grill. For instance, both chutney and savoury crumbs need only to be spread on the fish for the last minute of grilling.

METHOD

1 On a large, non-stick grilling tray lay out the salmon, cod and mackerel pieces, allowing a small space between each one and leaving space for the addition of oysters later.

2 Brush each piece with a little oil and grill for eight minutes.

3 Turn down the grill to medium.

4 Spread the mushroom butter in equal quantities on the salmon pieces, the tapenade on the cod pieces and the harissa-flavoured tomato salsa on the mackerel pieces.

5 Loosen the oysters from their shell bases and then top each one with equal amounts of pesto.

6 Place the oysters on the grilling tray with the fish and grill again for another three minutes.

7 Diners should receive a piece of each fish plus an oyster, ensuring that all the grill juices are distributed fairly.

WINE

A Muscadet (white)

Previous pages: Drimcong Fish Gri

Mussel and Dillisk Risotto

4 portions

♦ This risotto-cum-soup is dear to my heart. I love the pervasive salty-sea taste of dillisk. The use of seaweeds or sea vegetables as they are now often called is on the increase. Dillisk grows freely on the west coast of Ireland and has been harvested, wind- and sun-dried for centuries.

METHOD

1. Heat butter in a heavy-based saucepan.
2. Add onion and garlic and cook until soft – about two minutes.
3. Add rice. Mix and stir for a further minute.
4. Over a medium heat pour in the mixed wine and stock. Stir until absorbed and continue stirring in the liquid, ladle by ladle, until completely absorbed with the rice. This process takes 15-20 minutes by which time the rice should have a creamy texture and still have a bite to it.
5. Stir in the two tablespoons of parmesan or regato and keep warm.
6. Finish the dish by heating the 700 ml/1 pt stock in a large saucepan.
7. Chop dillisk roughly and add to stock.
8. Add the risotto and the mussels and bring to the boil.
9. Taste and season and serve in deep soup plates sprinkling the remaining Parmesan/regato and the chopped fennel equally over each portion.

WINE

A Verdiccio (white)

INGREDIENTS

FOR RISOTTO

50g/2oz butter

1 small onion, finely chopped

2 garlic cloves, crushed

175 g/6 oz arborio rice

150 ml/¼ pt dry white wine mixed with 850ml/1¼ pt hot fish stock

2 tbs parmesan or regato cheese, grated

25 g/1 oz dried dillisk, soaked for 5 minutes in cold water

700 ml/1 pt fish stock

48 large mussels, cleaned, steamed open and shelled (see p 46)

salt and ground black pepper

1 tbs Parmesan or regato cheese, grated

2 tbs fennel, finely chopped

Black and White Pudding with Apple Compôte

4 portions

2 tbs sunflower oil
4 x 50 g/2 oz slices black pudding
4 x 50 g/2 oz slices white pudding
more fresh thyme for garnish

FOR COMPÔTE
25 g/1 oz butter
1 medium onion, finely chopped
1 garlic clove, crushed
3 large cooking apples, peeled, cored
and chopped
150 ml/¼ pt medium dry white wine
sprig fresh thyme
salt and ground white pepper

METHOD

1 Make the compôte first by heating butter in a saucepan.

2 Cook onion and garlic in the butter for two minutes.

3 Add apple, wine, thyme and season.

4 Mix well, bring to the boil and then simmer, covered, for 15 minutes until thickened enough to mould on a plate.

5 Once made the compôte can be cooled, refrigerated and reheated when required.

6 Now complete the dish by heating the oil in a large frying pan and frying the slices of black and white pudding for two minutes each side over a medium heat.

7 On four warm serving plates build four individual towers of black and white pudding and apple compôte as follows:

> 2 tsp apple compôte
> 1 slice of white pudding
> 2 tsp apple compôte
> 1 slice of black pudding
> 2 tsp apple compôte

8 Garnish each portion with a sprig of thyme.

9 Serve with a meat gravy or apple and thyme sauce (see p 29).

WINE

A Pinot Gris from Alsace

The best and most appreciated children's food is stolen: spoonfuls of jam when nobody is looking, chunks of cheese nibbled in dark corners or under the sheets at bedtime, apples, the great treasure, from trees in forbidden orchards. Children are closer to the earth and nature. Consuming the bounty of clandestine forays to the fridge in hidden places makes them more so. I remember, as a child, sharing dinner with our pet cat under the stairs!

The children's recipes here are compiled from the multiple experiences of my own childhood, cooking as a chef who is also a father and, most importantly, the sense that as far as food taste is concerned my predilections are still childlike.

Coddle

♦ Coddle has long been a favourite in our family – a wonderfully quick one-pot dinner that appeals to children and adults alike.

METHOD

1 Put all ingredients except parsley and pepper in a saucepan and bring to the boil.
2 Cover and simmer for 20 minutes.
3 Add parsley and season with pepper.
4 Serve in deep soup plates.

INGREDIENTS

8 pork sausages, each cut in three

4 rashers, cut in thin strips

2 large potatoes,
cut in 5 cm/2 inch chunks

1 medium onion, finely chopped

2 medium carrots, sliced in thin rounds

700 ml/1 pt chicken or vegetable stock

2 tbs fresh parsley, finely chopped

ground white pepper

Sweet and Sour Drumsticks

4 portions
Oven: 220°C/425°F/gas mark 7

INGREDIENTS

1 tbs sunflower oil

8 chicken drumsticks ◄
– about 900 g/2 lb in total

salt and ground black pepper

**FOR SWEET AND SOUR SAUCE
MIX TOGETHER**

2 tsp Worcester sauce

2 tbs tomato ketchup

1 tbs grain mustard

1 tbs clear honey

2 tbs red wine vinegar

2 tsp rich dark soy sauce

3 tbs fresh orange juice

½ tsp ground ginger

2 garlic cloves, crushed

METHOD

1 Brush a roasting tin all over with oil. Lay the drumsticks side by side in the tin and season with salt and pepper.

2 Roast for 20 minutes.

3 While drumsticks are roasting heat the sauce but do not boil.

4 Turn the drumsticks and pour the sauce over them.

5 Roast again for 15 minutes by which time the drumsticks will show signs of caramelisation.

6 Serve with spoonfuls of sauce together with salad, rice or couscous.

OPTIONS ◄

Cold, these drumsticks make a good picnic item and the sauce is ideal for barbecues. Larger appetites may need more drumsticks and more sauce.

Nutty Burgers

4 portions

♦ These vegetarian burgers have a deceptively meaty taste – a good alternative to beef.

METHOD

1 In a large, deep pan fry onions in butter over medium heat for three minutes.

2 Add carrot and mushrooms and fry for five minutes more, stirring and mixing now and then.

3 Turn off heat and add breadcrumbs, nuts, parsley, egg and soy sauce.

4 Season with pepper and mix thoroughly.

5 When cool enough to handle, form four burgers by hand. They should measure approximately 7 cm/2¾ inch wide x 2.5 cm/1 inch thick. The burgers can be prepared to this stage and refrigerated until required.

6 Fry gently in hot oil for about five minutes each side.

7 Serve with tomato and fruit chutney (see p 122) or tomato ketchup.

INGREDIENTS

1 medium onion, finely chopped

50 g/2 oz soft butter

1 medium carrot, peeled and grated

175 g/6 oz mushrooms, sliced

75 g/3 oz brown breadcrumbs

175 g/6 oz cashew or mixture of nuts, finely chopped in a food processor

2 tbs fresh parsley, finely chopped

1 small egg, lightly beaten

1 tbs light soy sauce

ground black pepper

1 tbs sunflower oil

Fish Cakes

4 portions

450 g/1 lb cold cooked fish – such as ◄
cod and salmon

4 spring onions, finely chopped

1 cm/½ inch slice fresh root ginger,
finely chopped

3 small pickled gherkins, finely
chopped

5 tbs mayonnaise

75 g/3 oz fine white breadcrumbs

salt and ground white pepper

2 eggs

OPTIONS ◄

Any left-over cooked fish can be made
into fish cakes. They freeze well.

METHOD

1 Flake the fish and combine well with spring
onions, ginger, gherkins and mayonnaise.

2 Add 25 g/1 oz breadcrumbs and mix well.

3 Season.

4 Shape into eight cakes of about 6 cm/2½
inch diameter and 2.5 cm/1 inch thick.

5 Beat the eggs in a shallow bowl.

6 Dip fish cakes in egg and then in the
remaining breadcrumbs.

7 Refrigerate for at least an hour and then fry
for about 10 minutes, turning once, until
golden.

8 Serve with tuna mayonnaise (see p 114).

Tuna Pâté

METHOD

1 Process all the ingredients together in a food processor until blended and smooth.
2 Remove from processor with a spatula and refrigerate in a covered container.
3 Serve with toast, in a sandwich, on french bread or savoury biscuits. Use over a period of three to four days.

INGREDIENTS

1 x 200 g/7 oz can tuna in oil

25 g/1 oz soft butter

juice of half a lemon

25 g/1 oz fine white breadcrumbs

½ tsp harissa (see p 111) or chilli sauce

pinch of ground white pepper

Baked Bananas in Caramel Sauce

4 portions
Oven: 200°C/400°F/gas mark 6

INGREDIENTS

For caramel sauce
110 g/4 oz castor sugar
120 ml/4 fl oz water
275 ml/½ pt cream
4 peeled bananas
75 g/3 oz soft brown sugar
1 tsp cinnamon
25 g/1 oz butter, cut in six pieces
3 tbs fresh orange juice

OPTIONS ◄

Vanilla ice cream is a lovely cold foil to this hot dessert.

METHOD

1 Make caramel sauce by bringing sugar and water to the boil, without stirring, in a heavy-based saucepan over medium heat.

2 Continue boiling until the colour turns a golden caramel.

3 Take off the heat immediately and add the cream, holding the saucepan at arm's length to avoid being spattered with the hot liquid.

4 Return to a low heat and stir until smooth. Keep warm but do not boil again.

5 Finish by putting bananas in an ovenproof dish/casserole and sprinkle with sugar and cinnamon.

6 Drop butter pieces on top and pour on orange juice.

7 Bake for 15 minutes and serve with caramel sauce.

Facing page: Baked Bananas in Caramel Sauc

INDEX

scones

Smoked Salmon Scones, 95

Seafood Couscous, 48

Smoked Salmon, Warm, with Spinach Dressing, 20

Smoked Salmon Scones, 95

Sorbet, Apple and Lemon, 83

Soufflé, Hot Chocolate, in Sabayon Sauce, 90

soups

Cheese Soup with Celery Sticks, 13

Chinese Broth, 14

Pea Soup, 16

Spaghetti with Vegetables and Pesto, 55

Spiced Pork Roast, Apple and Thyme Cream Sauce, 29

Spinach Dressing, 20

Spinach Sauce, 53

stir-fries

Monk and Mussel Stir-Fry, 46

Pork and Vegetable Stir-Fry, 103

Stir-Fried Cabbage with Mushroom, Onion and Bacon, 78

Strawberry Gratin, 92

Sweet and Sour Drumsticks, 134

Sweet Pepper Marmalade, 34

Sweet Pepper Sauce, 34

Sweetcorn Pancakes with Crème Fraîche, Apple and Raspberry Sauce, 54

T

Tahini Sauce, 58

Tapenade, 112

tomatoes

Sautéed Cherry Tomatoes with Parsley and Thyme, 76

Tomato and Fruit Chutney, 122

Tomato and Onion Salad in Balsamic and Hazelnut Dressing, 66

Tomato Salsa, 56

Tomato Sauce, 120

Tuna Mayonnaise, 114

Tuna Pâté, 137

Turnip Bake, 73

V

vegetable dishes. see also individual vegetables

Carrot and Nut Terrine, 58

Chickpea Cakes, 56

Chinese Broth, 14

Couscous with Vegetables, 60

Couscous with Vegetables, Nuts and Dried Fruit, 60

Nutty Burgers, 135

Ratatouille, 125

Rice Balls with Pepper Compôte, 59

Ricotta and Walnut Dumplings, 53

Spaghetti with Vegetables and Pesto, 55

Sweetcorn Pancakes, 54

Venison, Burgundy, 106

Vinaigrette, 24

W

Warm Smoked Salmon with Spinach Dressing, 20

Y

Yoghurt and Orange Dressing, 68

Z

Zabaglione, 90